Unlocking Success
for
Small Business

Seven Keys to Creating a Successful Company

Tom Cremer

Unlocking Success for Small Business

Published in the United States

First Edition

January 1, 2011

ISBN—13: 978-1453744581

ISBN—10: 1453744584

Cover Photo: Rolff Images at Fotolia.com

Contents

Preface

I began my career as a management trainee for a large manufacturing company, worked hard, and rose through the ranks. After a rewarding career, I walked away when I was at the top of my game as a vice president for a Fortune 500 company and become a consultant.

I thought I knew what I was doing when I launched my first company, but the truth is that I just had good timing. A monkey with a sharp stick could have done what I did and made money. My expertise as a business consultant was in demand, and companies were paying top dollar for advice in my field of expertise—supply chain management. The next ten years proved to be a wild and wonderful ride.

At the height of my success, I decided to reinvent myself and create a new, more streamlined organization to increase my profitability. I thought I was doing everything right, but I crashed and burned within a year. I had no idea what went wrong. There was, however, one thing of which I was certain—the failure was not *my* fault.

Instead of critically analyzing my own performance, I did what many people do—I looked for someone or something to blame. I blamed the economy, my associates, my banker, and even my customers. The truth is, although I was skilled in my field of expertise, I actually knew very little about managing all of the complex intricacies of a complete company.

Rather than taking time to reflect on my failure, I jumped right back into the game and started a new company. This time, I took a different approach and followed my passion. I always wanted to work in the field of graphic arts. Armed with this passion, I believed that I had created such outstanding products that they would sell themselves, unfortunately that was not the case.

As a result, this venture produced the same outcome—failure. I was stumped. As a consultant, I made millions of dollars for my clients, yet when it came to running my own company, I could not understand what I was doing wrong.

Before starting another business, I decided to do something different. I dedicated myself to learning all that I could about operating a business successfully. I was not interested in the mechanics of starting a company, such as how to set up QuickBooks or where to obtain a tax ID number; I wanted to know what *real* people did to succeed.

In preparation for this journey, I began by reviewing my personal library. As it turned out, I was sitting on a proverbial gold mine. Being a compulsive note taker, I had filled over seventy-five diaries with detailed notes on the companies with whom I had worked during my career. I had traveled throughout the United States, Europe, Asia, and South Africa and worked closely with over five hundred companies.

I spent an entire year reviewing my notes, recording observations, and conducting interviews with some of the key executives with whom I had worked. *Unlocking Success for Small Business* is a compilation of the lessons I learned working with some of the most successful companies in the world.

Section One

Research

Chapter 1

Research Methodology

The subject of success and failure of small businesses has intrigued me for years. I have marveled at companies that prospered in spite of overwhelming obstacles and scratched my head in disbelief at others that had everything going for them yet failed for no apparent reason.

When attempting to explain success, you often hear simplistic expressions such as:

- ➢ "Right time, right place."
- ➢ "The product sold itself."
- ➢ "Luck of the draw."

Conversely when explaining failure, many owners use the following:

- ➢ "The economy did me in."
- ➢ "The big guys don't play fair."
- ➢ "Washington makes it impossible for small companies to succeed."

Rarely does anyone take personal responsibility for failure. Having worked with small companies for over twenty years, I felt that there was something else. I began my research with a single assumption and one basic goal.

Assumption:

There is a strong link between the personal behavior of owners and the performance of their companies.

If my assumption was correct, my goal was to identify specific behaviors that had the greatest effect on success and failure.

With that in mind, I developed the following process to conduct my research:

> ➢ Define success for small companies.
> ➢ Select a group of companies to study.
> ➢ Identify and analyze behaviors of owners that have a direct effect on success.

Definition of Success for a Small Company

For the purpose of this study, a small business is considered successful if it meets **all** of the following requirements:

> ➢ Be in operation a minimum of five years.
> ➢ Have generated profit for at least three of the five years.
> ➢ Be trending in a positive direction (continued profit).
> ➢ The profit for the business must be twice the annual salary that the owner could reasonably earn working for another company in a similar capacity.

The reason for this final requirement is to recognize the difference between a small business and a sole proprietorship. In order for a *business* to be successful, it needs to generate "wealth" of its own and not simply provide an income for the owner.

The Study Group

I decided to limit my study group to fifty companies that clearly fit the definition of success as well as fifty that had failed dramatically. My goal was to focus on companies that operated on the extremes of success and failure.

(Note: For expediency purposes, the two groups will be referred to as the SG and FG for success and failure groups.)

Behaviors

The next task was to identify behaviors, characteristics, or attributes that have the greatest impact on small companies. The ones I chose came from my experience of working with independent companies.

Characteristic

1. Accountability
2. Asset management
3. Business acumen
4. Commitment
5. Communication
6. Cost control
7. Creativity
8. Customer retention
9. Financial intelligence
10. Focus
11. General intelligence
12. Honesty
13. Human resource management
14. Marketing/advertising/promotion
15. Networking
16. Operational management
17. Passion
18. Planning

19. Political intelligence
20. Product knowledge
21. Product viability
22. Sales ability
23. Sense of urgency
24. Strategic vision
25. Detail orientation

Performance

In order to measure performance, each characteristic was rated, using the following scoring system:

+3 Performance at the highest possible level
+2 Significantly above average
+1 Slightly above
- 1 Slightly below
- 2 Significantly below average
- 3 Completely unacceptable performance

Ranking of Behaviors

The last step in the evaluation process was to compile the scores of the individual characteristic for all companies. The goal was to determine which characteristics had the greatest influence on success and failure.

The following are the rankings of the average scores for both groups:

	Success Group	Average Score
1.	Business acumen	2.98
2.	Product viability	2.98
3.	Sales ability	2.97
4.	Financial intelligence	2.96
5.	Focus	2.96
6.	Commitment	2.95

7.	Political intelligence	2.95
8.	Passion	2.94
9.	Cost control	2.91
10.	Planning	2.90
11.	Human resource management	2.88
12.	Customer retention	2.87
13.	Accountability	2.86
14.	Asset management	2.85
15.	Networking	2.84
16.	Product knowledge	2.83
17.	Sense of urgency	2.82
18.	Strategic vision	2.80
19.	General intelligence	2.79
20.	Marketing/advertising	2.77
21.	Creativity	2.75
22.	Operational management	2.71
23.	Communication	2.50
24.	Detail orientation	2.49
25.	Honesty	1.78

	Failure Group	Average Score
1.	Product knowledge	2.88
2.	General intelligence	2.80
3.	Honesty	2.52
4.	Passion	2.17
5.	Communication	1.88
6.	Creativity	1.78
7.	Marketing/advertising	1.48
8.	Networking	1.07
9.	Strategic vision	0.98
10.	Asset management	-1.19
11.	Sense of urgency	-1.28
12.	Accountability	-1.49
13.	Human resource management	-2.03
14.	Customer retention	-2.06
15.	Human resource management	-2.09
16.	Planning	-2.11
17.	Detail orientation	-2.13
18.	Cost control	-2.14
19.	Political intelligence	-2.17
20.	Focus	-2.19
21.	Sales ability	-2.21
22.	Commitment	-2.56
23.	Financial intelligence	-2.57
24.	Business acumen	-2.68
25.	Product viability	-2.71

It is important to keep in mind that the purpose of this study was not to rate the performance of individual companies or specific owners, but to identify the **behaviors** that had the greatest effect on the success and failure of small companies.

Coming up next...

Chapter 2 reveals the major lessons learned from the study.

Chapter 2

Seven Keys to Creating a Successful Company

The lessons learned from the study dramatically exceeded my expectations. Not only was I able to support my original assumption, I identified six other significant lessons. Any small business owner, or anyone thinking about starting a company, would be well served to know and understand the following keys.

Keys

1. There is a strong link between the personal behavior of owners and the success or failure of their companies.

2. Many people start companies for reasons that are not based on sound business or economic principles.

3. Many entrepreneurs grossly underestimate the amount of personal sacrifice required to create and sustain a successful company.

4. The performance levels required to be successful for an owner of a small company are much higher than those of a corporate manager.

5. In order for a small business to be successful, an owner must be good at many things outside of his or her area of expertise.

6. A great product alone is not enough to ensure success.

7. A small number of very specific behaviors have a dramatic effect on the success or failure of a small business.

The following is a closer look at each key lesson.

Key #1

There is a strong link between the personal behavior of owners and the success or failure of their companies.

Although I had strong feelings before conducting this study, it wasn't until I reviewed over a hundred companies that I came to the conclusion that the behavior of owners and the success or failure of their companies was virtually *inseparable*. Since the majority of the study group consisted of companies with less than one hundred employees and only one owner, it was relatively easy to identify the causes of success and failure.

My assumptions were supported by three major observations:

Positive Behavior and Success

When a company succeeded as a result of a particular characteristic, the owner was usually proficient (more than 87 percent of the cases) in the same area. For example, companies that were known for outstanding quality were owned by people with incredible product knowledge and strong attention to details.

Negative Behavior and Failure

Companies that failed for a particular reason were almost always (more than 92 percent of the cases) led by owners deficient in that same area. For example, companies that failed due to a lack of fiscal control were led by people who had difficulty managing their own finances.

Inconsistent Behaviors

Of all of the correlations, the most interesting was the fact few companies (less than 5 percent) in the SG succeeded in areas that were contrary to the personal behaviors or habits of the owners. For example, there were no companies that succeeded based on strong customer attraction, run by owners who were poor at sales.

It must be stressed that the focus of this research was on small, independently owned and operated companies. The influence of the owner diminishes as companies grow and take on additional staff. As new employees with specific skills are added, they compensate for deficiencies of the owners.

The importance of this lesson is that, until a company can afford to hire specialists, the owner must be proficient in all aspects of operating a business (see Key #5).

Key #2

Many people start companies for reasons that are *not* based on sound business or economic principles.

There is a certain mystique that attracts many people to start their own company. Some owners are more in love with the idea of being the boss and having a big office, rather than taking responsibility for the day-to-day operation of an entire business.

The following were the most common reasons identified by the FG for starting their companies:

- ➤ The desire to be their own boss
- ➤ Freedom to set their own work schedule
- ➤ Hate taking orders

> ➢ Boredom with current job
> ➢ Lack of career advancement
> ➢ Forced into business due to unemployment
> ➢ Desire to promote a personal agenda

Conversely, the following were the most common reasons identified by the SG for founding their companies:

> ➢ The creation of a completely new or unique product
> ➢ Dramatically improved an existing product
> ➢ Discovered a niche market not being served
> ➢ To seize an opportunity due to the demise of a competitor
> ➢ To build an organization around the specific skills of a unique person or team of people

Although there are no guarantees, companies based on sound economic reasons have a higher chance for success than ones created to satisfy the personal desires of an owner.

Key #3

Many entrepreneurs grossly underestimate the amount of personal sacrifice required to create and sustain a successful company.

Before starting a business, it is important to understand the level of commitment and sacrifice required for success. When a person is part of a large corporation, he or she is only responsible for a specific area of the operation. Owners, however, are responsible for everything.

Their duties do not end at 5:00 p.m., and problems never take a holiday. Owners cannot call in sick, even when they are ill; they are never on vacation, even when they are thousands of miles away from their office; and they can never say, "That's not my job!" even when it is out of their area of expertise.

Over 48 percent of the owners in the FG admitted that they were not prepared for the amount of work that ownership entailed. Within that same group, over half claimed that the allure of increased income offered by ownership was not worth the sacrifices required.

The luster of ownership wore off quickly for many new owners once they realized the amount of personal sacrifice required to operate a company.

On a personal note…

I am as guilty of this as anyone. I attributed a great deal of my success, while working for large companies, on my strong work ethic. However, nothing I did as a manager came close to the amount of personal sacrifice I made operating my own company.

I always laugh when people say they want to start their own business so they can name their own hours. I simply smile and say, "I can tell you exactly what they will be: 7 x 24 x 365!"

Key #4

The performance levels required to be successful for an owner of a small company are much higher that those of a corporate manager.

Over 68 percent of the businesses that failed were led by people who had successful careers in large corporations. When a person is part of a large organization, they have extensive support networks to assist them with most administrative functions. As a result, they can focus all of their attention on their own job.

Small business owners, on the other hand, are responsible for everything, including areas in which they have no interest or experience. Not only do they not like performing these tasks, but they tend to do them poorly and they divert precious time and energy away from more pressing issues. As a result, many owners become overwhelmed and frustrated by the magnitude of administrative tasks and often lose focus on the high-level goals and objectives required to make the business successful.

Key #5

In order for a small business to be successful, an owner must be good at many things outside of his or her area of expertise.

Independent business owners must be proficient in the following areas:

Accounting:
 ➢ General accounting
 ➢ Cash flow management
 ➢ Accounts receivable and payable
 ➢ Payroll & Taxes

Human Resources
 ➢ Recruiting
 ➢ Hiring and firing
 ➢ Training and development
 ➢ Compensation, insurance, and benefits

Supply-Chain Management
- Procurement
- Inventory control
- Contract management
- Supplier qualification and inspection

Logistics
- Transportation
- Shipping and receiving
- Warehousing and distribution

Manufacturing
- Production planning and quality control
- Product design
- Production engineering
- Maintenance

Technology
- Hardware management
- Software support
- Telecommunications

Sales
- Prospecting
- Contract negotiations
- Relationship management
- Customer service

Just to name a few.

Mastery of all of these is virtually impossible for one person, but the study indicated that the higher the number of areas of proficiency, the greater the chance for success. For example, 83 percent of the SG scored high (2.0 plus) in five of the seven major categories.

On the other hand, less than 16 percent of the FG scored high (2.0 plus) in five or more categories. I do not attribute this to intellectual ability because the study revealed that the two groups scored almost identically in general intelligence. My interviews suggest that the problem resides in interest levels.

Many owners in the FG were convinced that if they did *their* job well, everything else would take care of itself. This was especially true of people who were skilled in product-related areas, such as design and development. There was a common belief among the FG that if their products were good enough, they would sell themselves, which leads to the next key.

Key #6

A great product alone is not enough to ensure success.

All of the owners in the study had great pride in what they sold; however, many in the FG put undue attention on products at the expense of other business issues. On the surface, it makes sense to focus considerable energy in this area; however, my research indicates that good products alone cannot ensure success. It was interesting to note that almost 70 percent of the failed companies sold similar products that were successful with other companies.

While most of the owners in the SG claimed to have built their companies around their products, more than half admitted to spending more time on other functions, such as finance, marketing, advertising, and sales, than they did on product-related functions.

Operating a successful company is more than just pumping out a bunch of high quality widgets.

Key #7

A small number of very specific behaviors have a dramatic effect on the success or failure of a small business.

This final element was so surprising that I dedicated the rest of my research to its study. I am convinced that there is no coincidence that the seven highest rated behaviors in the success group were the same seven lowest rated for the owners who failed. This means that the characteristics that have the greatest influence over success *also* have the most dramatic impact on failure.

What further amazed me was that their negative powers are so strong that poor performance in any single area could cause an entire company to fail. This effect is so powerful that I refer to them as fatal flaws.

Coming up next…

Chapter 3 focuses on the power and influence of the behaviors that have the greatest impact on success and failure of small companies.

Chapter 3

Critical Behaviors for Success

I came upon the critical behaviors for success in a curious way. As I reviewed the two groups, seven behaviors consistently ranked at the top for successful owners. It wasn't until I focused on the failure group that I discovered that poor performance in the same seven were the major cause for the demise of their companies.

The most significant finding was that not only did these behaviors account for the majority of failures, but the research indicated that poor performance in any *single* characteristic could lead to the complete failure of an entire organization.

As a result, I came to the conclusion that, due to the powerful influence that owners have on their companies, they not only have to be good in *all* seven key characteristics, but they cannot be bad in any *one*.

The characteristics that have the greatest influence over both the success, and failure, of small companies are:

> * Product viability
> * Business acumen
> * Sales ability
> * Financial intelligence
> * Political intelligence
> * Focus
> * Commitment

Product Viability

Product viability is not a personal characteristic, but rather, it is the ability of an owner to create a product that is commercially successful. In order for a product to be viable, it needs to meet the following three conditions:

1. It must satisfy a real need.
2. Customers must be willing to pay to have that need satisfied.
3. The price that customers are willing to pay must cover all expenses and generate an acceptable level of profit.

No matter what a company does, it is of no value if their products do not generate profits. A company could have the best people, superb quality, and an outstanding location, but it means nothing unless customers perceive a need for their products and are willing to pay a reasonable price.

Owners who fail to realize that their products are not viable are destined to fail. Absolutely nothing can compensate for lack of customer interest, or worse yet, interest only at a price that results in a loss.

See chapter 4 for case studies on product viability.

Business Acumen

Business acumen can be described as *quickness, accuracy, and keenness of judgment*; or *insight in business matters*. The ability to clearly understand complex business issues in order to make profitable business decisions is the leading personal behavior of successful owners.

Business acumen should not be confused with general intelligence or product knowledge. Successful owners must have a comprehensive understanding of the market, their competition, and the economy, along with strong powers of observation.

Successful business leaders know how to read complex situations and are able to use their insight to make profitable decisions.

See chapter 5 for case studies on business acumen.

Sales Ability

Selling is not limited to the exchange of goods and services. A person's ability to sell themselves, and their ideas, is critical to success in any field. Successful people know how to get their message across and realize that they have to engage clients on a personal level before they can convert them to customers.

Over 42 percent of owners in the FG admitted to having problems selling. Unfortunately, many owners have a poor opinion of the sales profession based on old stereotypes. In fact, 35 percent claimed that they did not view "sales" as a real profession. These owners believed that sales people were not necessary if their products were good enough.

Unfortunately, they did not understand that the old adage, *"Build a better mousetrap and the world will beat a path to your door,"* is no longer true. The Internet and the global economy have changed everything. Today's consumers have unlimited choices at the click of a mouse.

Vigorous sales programs are critical for all small companies. Successful owners do not wait for business to come to them; they actively go out and engage their customers.

See chapter 6 for case studies on sales ability.

Financial Intelligence

Successful business owners have great respect and appreciation for the role of finance. They make it a priority to learn as much as they can. Even after they have hired professional financial managers, they continue to take an active role in all financial decisions.

Successful owners base all expenditures on sound economic justification and true business needs. Decisions are not made on unfounded opinions or personal feelings.

Conversely, not only do many unsuccessful owners have a limited understanding of finance, but some are openly hostile toward any attempt to place controls on their financial decisions. Many like to "rule by their gut," preferring to make decisions on emotion rather than facts.

Over 56 percent of the FG had difficulty controlling their spending. The most common areas of failure to exercise sound business judgments were in expenditures on lavish offices, needless travel, extravagant entertainment, and unnecessary staffing.

Financial resource management represents one of the clearest areas of separation in philosophy between the two groups. The SG clearly differentiated between "personal vs. business" money, while most of the FG owners saw no difference. In fact, many in the FG had an "entitlement" perspective regarding their company's assets. These owners believed that their ability to spend as they saw fit was one of the "rights of ownership."

Unfortunately, no other characteristic can compensate for poor financial decision making.

See chapter 7 for case studies on financial intelligence.

Political Intelligence

Successful business people accept the fact that politics are everywhere. They understand how things *really* work, as opposed to how they feel they *should* work, and use their political insight to their advantage. Knowing how to use the system is critical to success.

Unsuccessful owners do poorly at politics for two main reasons: they either are not aware of the politics that affect their business, or they dislike them so much that they attempt to fight back. In either case, the failure to accept political reality is futile. The people with the strongest feelings about what they perceive to be right and wrong seem to have the greatest difficulty in highly political environments.

The popular Hollywood notion of the maverick that stands up for his or her principles and ultimately defeats the political establishment is typically not true in business. People who fight the system rarely succeed in the real business world.

See chapter 8 for case studies on political intelligence.

Focus

Successful owners take their role seriously and focus 100 percent of their time and energy on their companies. Many make running their business the highest priority in their life, even to the extreme of placing business over family, friends, and personal interests.

The ability to stay on task was a problem for 42 percent of the FG, while 84 percent of the successful group (SG) scored high in this area. Struggling companies often bounce from priority to priority in search of success. Like an attention deficit teenager, unsuccessful owners start many projects, but finish very few.

Excessive changes in direction cause small companies to burn massive amounts of limited resources. Many unsuccessful owners lose focus when things get tough, while others simply have a wandering eye. When attractive new alternatives come along, they drop everything and chase a new direction.

See chapter 9 for case studies on focus.

Commitment

True commitment separates winners from losers. It is no surprise that successful people are extremely committed to what they do for a living. It wasn't until I compared the two groups that I understood why highly committed people are more successful.

People who commit more time and energy have a better understanding of what is going on within their company, their products, the marketplace, and the economy. This higher level of insight gives them a tremendous competitive advantage.

People who are not totally committed tend to do just enough to get by and, as a result, are unable to compete against highly driven competitors.

See chapter 10 for case studies on commitment.

In Conclusion

Of all of the things I learned, the dramatic impact of fatal flaws caught me by surprise. While most small business owners realize they have to be good at many things to succeed, few understand the catastrophic effects of poor performance in these few behaviors.

Coming up next...

Chapters 4 through 10 feature case studies that illustrate the powerful impact of these behaviors on success and the devastating effects of fatal flaws.

Section 2

Case Studies

Although these cases are based on real events, the names of the characters and companies have been changed. Any similarity to actual people, places, or organizations is strictly coincidental.

Each chapter is divided into two sections—the wrong and right way to perform the behavior being featured. The wrong way represents the fatal flaw, while the right way features outstanding performance by successful entrepreneurs.

Chapter 4

Case Studies on Product Viability

Wrong way: The Amazing Custom Software Company

Background

This case took place during the early 1990s at the beginning of the electronic commerce revolution. During that time, literally hundreds of companies were competing to get a piece of an emerging multibillion dollar market.

Not only were software developers involved in the frenzy, but investors of all types were jumping on the bandwagon. Companies were springing up overnight with millions of dollars in financial backing based on vague business propositions. Some companies did not even have a product to sell, and still they had investors. In fact, a new term was created to explain this phenomena—it was called "vaporware."

The goal was to develop something attractive enough for investors to support and customers to buy. Vaporware, however, did absolutely nothing; it just simulated what the proposed product would do eventually. As crazy as this sounds, it actually worked for a brief period of time. Things were moving so fast in the high-stakes world of e-commerce that no one wanted to be left behind.

I was hired by the investment firm that funded the Amazing Custom Software Company (ACSC). As excited as they were about the potential of the product, one of the board members wanted hard financial proof to support their investment. My job was to cut through the hype and quantify the actual profit potential of the product being developed.

The job turned out to be quite challenging because the founder took great pride in his product and did not like anyone questioning any aspect of his business.

The Story

The founder of ACSC was a brilliant young programmer who created an extremely specialized piece of software. The goal was to link different commercial Web sites together into one common format and make e-commerce easier to use for high-volume corporate and industrial buyers.

Not only was Jason (the founder) a great software designer, he was a gifted presenter. He was able to create such powerful stories about his product that he raised over $5,000,000 before he sold his first copy. Although he could mesmerize audiences on exciting subjects such as artificial intelligence, he had a dark side; he was very intimidating.

Whenever he was confronted with dissenting opinions, he would cut his opponents down with severe verbal attacks. He did not like anyone questioning his intelligence and took great delight in publicly humiliating anyone who disagreed with him. His final rebuke to anyone who would not concede to him was, "*You* just don't get it." The implication was obvious. Most people, including his investors, were so intimidated that they simply gave in.

I became suspicious when Jason continually dodged my questions regarding the number of actual customers who had committed to buying his product. The majority of the board of directors was so captivated that they gave him a free pass;

however, after the first year concluded without any sales, they began to ask questions. Jason blamed all of the problems on the sales department and fired the entire sales force.

He honestly believed that his product was so good that it could sell itself, so he took matters into his own hands and hit the road. He was convinced that all he had to do was to demonstrate his software and customers would immediately buy.

Within a week, Jason's excursion into the world of sales generated a harsh lesson. Although he could intimidate employees and investors, he had no power over customers. Outside the four walls of his office, he was just another software salesman. Not only did buyers not drop to their knees and praise his brilliance, but most wouldn't give him the time of day. There were hundreds of similar products on the market, and customers did not see anything special about his software.

In order to buy more time from the board, Jason initiated a strategy that desperate companies often use to inflate their sales figures; i.e., he gave products away. When he told the board that he had a dozen beta test sites (customers), he was technically correct, but not exactly honest. Although it was true that twelve companies had received his software, only one bothered to install it, three returned it, and the rest showed absolutely no interest.

Jason's intention was not to deceive his investors; he was just trying to buy some time. He honestly felt he had created something so special that the world would beat a path to his door, once they learned of its brilliance. He was convinced that the problem was not his product—it was his customers. "They just didn't get it."

But as time passed without any hard sales, I was instructed by a senior board member to conduct a survey to determine the true potential of the product. The outcome was shocking.

Although the software was visually pleasing, it lacked one ingredient for success; it did not solve any problem. The best analogy was that Jason had perfected a way to make ice cubes at the North Pole.

I interviewed fifty potential clients and asked them two simple questions:

Question #1

On a scale of 0–10, with 0 being "absolutely no problem," and 10 being "catastrophic," how much of a problem is … (*what Jason's software claimed to do*)… for your company?

> **Answer:** 82 percent rated the problem at **ZERO**.

Of the 18 percent that responded with some degree above zero, I asked a second question:

Question #2

How much would you be willing to spend to solve the problem?

> **Answer:** 67 percent were willing to spend up to $500. None were willing to spend more than $1000.

The asking price for the amazing custom mainframe software was **$1,200,000 per corporate license.**

Although the investors were initially mesmerized by Jason's brilliance, his time was up. He was called before the board and was told that his services were no longer needed. The security guards told me that as they escorted him to his car, he looked back at the building and said, "They just don't get it."

Right way: The Opportunistic Plastic Distribution Company

Background

Gary was a classic rags-to-riches story. He worked his way through college loading trucks at a large plastics distribution company. After graduation, he was offered a sales position and worked his way up the corporate ladder. Within ten years, he was running the company.

Gary hired me to conduct an analysis of his sales program. He wanted to know all of the steps required to take a customer from what he called "need identification through need resolution." His goal was to improve his internal process to increase customer satisfaction.

I was impressed with Gary's level of commitment. He was not doing this to satisfy a corporate mandate; he honestly wanted to know how he could improve customer service. Even though he ran the top company in the market, he wanted to be better.

Unfortunately, Gary's tenure came to an abrupt end. Although he loved his job, he became frustrated with the bureaucracy of his parent company, a large financial conglomerate. The straw that broke the camel's back was a letter that was sent to hundreds of Gary's customers (without his knowledge) telling them that their business was no longer welcome. Apparently their sales volume was too low to meet the minimum acceptable levels of the parent company.

Gary's response to this action was to drive to the corporate headquarters and tell the CEO exactly what he thought of his new program. An hour later he was clearing out his office.

This is Gary's story.

The Story

Gary had a tremendous reputation in the business community, and soon after leaving his position, he assembled a group of local investors. He didn't have a glamorous slide presentation; he simply showed them a list of the customers that his former employer fired and said, "I want to get them back."

The investors loved what they heard and gave him $50,000 to get started. He built an efficient distribution company that focused on the needs of smaller customers. He rented an abandoned warehouse for a song and hired his former assistant to manage the office while he personally visited every customer who received a "Dear John" letter.

As it turned out, Gary was sitting in the perfect position. He knew everything about his competition, including their marketing plans, operating costs, distribution networks, and pricing strategies. He used his insight to build an effective operation that created profits in areas where larger companies lost money. By keeping his overhead costs to a bare minimum, he was able to generate respectable profits selling to small customers.

As his business grew, Gary was able to redefine his product. Rather than just selling plastic sheets, rods, and tubing, he sold "polymer solutions." His incredible product knowledge made him a valuable resource for his customers. He worked closely with engineers on major projects, such as home drainage systems. Instead of getting orders for twenty-five pieces of pipe, he won contracts to provide complete sewerage systems for large housing projects.

Gary's business doubled in size every six months, and within two years, he began receiving offers to buy his company. He turned everyone down until a large corporation made him an offer that he could not refuse. When all the dust had settled, he cleared over $3,000,000 on the sale of his company.

The press release announcing the acquisition said it best, *"The acquisition of the Opportunistic Plastic Distribution Company will provide a competitive advantage by maximizing our product offerings in key SMMS's"* (Strategic Minimal Market Segments, i.e., corporate speak for small customers).

The irony is that the conglomerate that acquired his company was the third restructuring of his former employer. None of the new management team had any idea they had just bought back the customers they had fired a couple years earlier.

Chapter 5

Case Studies on Business Acumen

"Jon isn't a real businessman; he just plays one at work."
An old friend

Business acumen: quickness, accuracy, and keenness of judgment; insight in business matters.

Wrong way: Play Business Incorporated

Background

The case of Play Business Incorporated comes from one of my more colorful clients. I was hired by the lead character's father to advise his son on procurement, inventory management, and expense control. Jon Sr. had a vested interest because he had convinced a group of friends to put up the original investment of over $500,000 to launch the company.

Although he had faith in his son's intelligence, he had serious concerns about his ability to manage his finances. His concerns were not unfounded.

While this case demonstrates poor performance in the area of commitment, the primary lesson learned from this example is what happens when an otherwise intelligent person has no grasp of how business really works, i.e., business acumen.

The Story

Jon Jr. was the VP of strategic business development (SBD) for a large financial institution. He had one of those unique jobs that only exist at extremely large and bureaucratic organizations. No one knew exactly what the VP of SBD actually did, but it sounded impressive, and he enjoyed a great deal of exposure to senior management. In reality, he had no real duties or responsibilities other than writing position papers for the president.

Jon came from wealth and privilege. His father and grandfather were CEOs of major corporations, and his mother sat on the boards of many business and charitable organizations. Jon attended great schools but didn't study anything related to business. He had a master's degree in art history but claimed that his true expertise was *insight*. He professed to have a gift of "seeing what others failed to perceive."

Despite living a charmed life, Jon was restless. He wasn't content making a six-figure salary for little effort; he wanted to run a company. He felt it was his destiny to be a CEO.

The president of Jon's company liked him and took him under his wing. Everyone assumed he was being groomed for bigger and better things. Although he was the youngest vice president in the company's history, he could not wait to take control, so at the ripe old age of twenty-six, his impatience drove him to move on.

Jon had no idea what he wanted to do, other than the fact that he *had* to be the CEO of a company; but not just any company—it had to fit the image he had carefully crafted for himself. He eventually found what he thought was the perfect opportunity in a promotional products company. The owner had fallen on hard times and was forced to sell at a significant loss.

Jon liked the company because the products were fun. They made T-shirts, pens, calendars, coffee mugs, and some creative marketing trinkets. He also heard that there were lots of opportunities to attend exciting conventions, combined with junkets to Asia to visit suppliers.

According to Jon's research, all the company needed was an "executive presence" (whatever that meant), and he was just the right person for the job. But contrary to what he believed, the only thing the company really needed was a few more customers. The operation was well run and had a loyal customer base.

The factory was situated in a poor section of town, but in spite of its location, the company benefited by having an strong workforce. The employees worked hard and appreciated having a job. Turnover was nonexistent, and there was actually a waiting list to get in.

Being in a low-rent district, the building was not pretty, but it was structurally sound and extremely functional. The equipment was old, but reliable and easy to maintain. The facility didn't have to be glamorous because customers never visited the factory, but Jon decided that he had to change everything. He needed something more representative of his "persona."

So, armed with big plans and borrowed funds, he moved the factory to a beautiful suburban business complex—complete with fountains, bicycle paths, and open-air cafés. To remove the stigma of a "factory," he installed an indoor running track, six jumbo screen televisions, and a latte bar. Since he didn't want to trash the place with greasy old machines, he bought all new state-of-the-art computer-controlled equipment.

Unfortunately, the new equipment presented a problem that Jon missed. The PC-driven machines were sophisticated and required a different type of employee to keep them running. Instead of minimum wage laborers, Jon had to hire highly trained computer technicians. Not only were they expensive, but they were hard to find and would leave on a moment's notice for a better job. However, finding technicians was only the tip of his HR problems.

In his attempt to create a new image for his company, Jon did not want to transfer the inner-city factory workers from the previous owners. His only concern was how he could fire everyone without getting sued. What he didn't realize was that the new factory was as easy to get to as Outer Mongolia for the employees. Few had cars, and those who did could not afford the gas to get to work.

The old adage "Be careful what you wish for!" struck home for Jon. As hard as it was to get hi-tech maintenance engineers, it was virtually impossible to find anyone who would work for $5.00 an hour in this affluent location. The local kids would never consider working in a factory, even when Jon doubled the pay to $10.00 per hour.

If all that wasn't bad enough, the few orders he inherited from the previous owner were cancelled due to production delays caused by the move. Within six months, Jon was broke and was forced to shut down the operation. With all of his investors' money being spent on moving the factory and buying new equipment, he did what he had done so many times before; he went to his parents for help.

Help came from one of his father's friends at his country club. Chip was the son of the club's treasurer. Jon didn't know much about him because he and his family were "recent" members. The term "recent" had negative connotations of new money, as opposed to Jon's rich family heritage, but he was willing to give Chip a chance and let him buy into his company.

Jon assumed that since Chip's parents belonged to the club, they must have a reasonable amount of money. What he didn't know was that Chip made all of his own money and got nothing from his parents. In fact, it was the other way around; his parents were living off *his* money. While it was true that his money was "new" money, it was also true that he had lots of it.

The reason Jon knew little about Chip was because Chip didn't spend much time at the club. Although his parents appeared to live there, Chip was never around. The few events he attended, he never mixed or mingled; in fact, he looked uncomfortable in the country club setting.

What no one knew was that although he looked like a preppy, he had the heart of a street fighter. He purposely cultivated an easy-going image to lure his competitors into overconfidence. In reality, he was a "turn-and-burn" expert who specialized in buying distressed companies, gutting them of waste, returning them to profitability, and selling them for huge profits.

Jon didn't know this when he took Chip on as a partner. He assumed that Chip had more money than he knew what to do with, and in his self-centered world, he actually thought that Chip was just parking some cash in his company as a friend.

The meeting between Jon and Chip that changed the course of the company took place over cocktails at the country club. Jon began by presenting an overview on his vision of the perfect company—the one *he* was building.

Chip had reviewed the financials in great detail prior to the meeting. He listening to Jon's ramblings for some time and then finally came right to the point: "How much do you need for me to become part of your company?" Jon glibly shot him a number.

Chip produced a document from his coat pocket and wrote in a number twice as high as Jon's request. As he was filling in the amount, he casually mentioned that the agreement was just a standard form that he always used when investing in a company. Jon jumped at the opportunity and signed without reading it. He wanted to move quickly before Chip could change his mind.

Jon's mind raced in anticipation of all of the things he could buy with the new infusion of cash. The first major purchase he was going to make was to buy a boat to entertain customers.

The two men shook on the deal and toasted to the success of the new company. Jon was so proud of the way he handled Chip that he never bothered to have the contract reviewed by his attorney. As he drove home that night, he couldn't help but laugh at how naïve Chip was; it proved to him that he was all "show and no go."

Jon was in such a good mood that he took a couple of days off to celebrate his success. When he finally returned to the office, he was shocked to see Chip's Mercedes parked in his (Jon's) space. The office door was open, and he could hear Chip on the phone. Chip waived him in, but he made no attempt to finish the call.

Jon's beautiful office was in shambles. His custom furniture was covered with coffee cups, soda cans, pizza boxes, and candy wrappers. His hand-painted mural had been destroyed by the spreadsheets that had been stapled to the walls, and his beautiful glass coffee table looked like it was about to burst under the weight of a massive copier. But of all of the possible questions racing through Jon's mind, all he could think of was how Chip got in the building; he had never given him a key.

When Chip finally finished his call, he said, "Welcome, partner," and went into an energetic speech about his plans for the new company. He fired up a series of detailed financial statements on one of the giant screens he had removed from the running track.

Jon was stunned—unable to speak. He didn't know what to make of his new partner, so he just sat quietly and listened. Chip's attention to detail caught him by surprise. He thought it was ridiculous that a millionaire should be worried about every nickel and dime expenditure. What he didn't realize was that his attention to detail was exactly why he was a millionaire.

Jon assumed that Chip was just trying to create a good impression and that his enthusiasm would wear off by lunch. But to his surprise, they worked straight through the day, finishing close to midnight. Jon was exhausted, but Chip looked like he was just getting started.

Before leaving, Jon asked the one question he had been dying to ask all day, "When will you deposit your check into my account?" Chip flashed his trademark smile and said, "I don't want you to worry about money. I'll take care of you." The way the question was asked, and the way the response was phrased, was a prediction of their future relationship.

The rest of the week was a repeat of Monday. The only thing that kept Jon going was the promise of Chip's check, but when Friday arrived and the funds were still not received, he began to panic. Jon suddenly came to the conclusion that he had been too nice for too long—it was time to show Chip who was in charge. Besides, he had big plans for the weekend; he was going shopping for a new boat.

At 5:00 p.m., he straightened his tie, took a deep breath, and said, "I think we have covered everything. It's time to move forward." He extended his hand and said, "I must get to the bank before they close. I need your check *now*!"

Chip stared at him like he was speaking Chinese—to be more precise, like he was standing on his head, juggling flaming bowling balls, and speaking Chinese. After a long pause, he said, "I told you before—I don't want you to worry about money. That's my job. Give me the checkbook. I'll make the deposit, you take the weekend off, and we'll hit it again on Monday."

Perhaps he was delirious from the long hours, but that was all Jon needed to hear. He got his allowance, was let out of school early, and didn't have any homework. Life was sweet.

The weekend of testing new boats was just what the doctor ordered. It gave Jon time to sort things out and put them in the proper perspective. He was pleased with the way he had handled things and marveled at his brilliance for letting Chip think he was in charge.

Jon was so self-absorbed that he naively assumed he had seen the last of Chip, so he was in no hurry to get to the office on Monday. He arrived around 10:00 a.m. and was surprised to see four unmarked black cargo vans in front of the building.

The office was a beehive of activity. Chip was standing on a ladder shouting orders through a bull horn. He and his crew of a dozen young men were dressed in black from head to toe. They looked like commandos breaking into a bank. It was clear that they had worked all weekend because the building was completely gutted. His beautiful office was gone, and his custom-made mahogany desk was being used as a workbench on the loading dock.

Jon was too shocked to say a word, but it wouldn't have been of any use, because Chip was on a roll. When he finally noticed Jon he shouted, "Dig in. This is going to be fun." Obviously Chip's idea of fun was completely different than his.

By the end of the week, Jon was a complete wreck. His back was sore, his knees hurt, and his hands were covered with blisters. This was not what he signed up for, but he had a much bigger problem; Chip had still not deposited his check.

Friday became showdown time again, and Jon waited until five o'clock before taking Chip aside. He nervously cleared his throat and said, "We need to talk about my salary!" He began rambling on about his financial obligations, his hard work, and even attempted to explain the powerful position he had before starting the company, all of which came across like whining.

Chip jumped up and said, "What the hell are you talking about? *You're an owner*. You don't get a salary! Those guys (pointing to the workers) get a salary. You get what's left over—they are called *profits*, and the last time I looked, you are almost $1,000,000 in the hole." He concluded by saying, "I suggest you get back to work. Those trucks aren't going to unload themselves." Jon finally had enough and stormed out.

He walked around the complex for an hour before working up enough courage to confront Chip again. He returned and said, "We need to talk." He launched into a rambling monologue about entitlement. Chip cradled his chin in his hands and pretended to be listening.

When Jon was finished, Chip handed him a one page financial statement and calmly said, "Pay close attention." As Chip reviewed the numbers, the blood began to drain from Jon's face. Chip concluded by saying, "The bottom line is this—you won't see a dime until this place starts to make a profit, and the way you've been running things, that will never happen. With my help, it will be profitable in three to five years. So you have to ask yourself, how long you can live without a paycheck?" Jon looked like he was hit by a train.

Chip finished him off by saying, "Without my money, this place goes right into bankruptcy, and you won't collect a penny. Besides, the way you have handled the books, you will spend the next ten years fighting investor lawsuits. You have two choices— you can either roll up your sleeves and go back to work, or you can sign this (he placed a new contract on the table) and walk away free and clear of all debts and lawsuits."

Jon's stomach was on fire, and his knees were so weak that he had to sit down. His mind was searching for option #3, but there was none. A flood of emotions hit him like a tsunami. The thought of lawsuits and massive debt was overwhelming. He knew he was finished, so he signed the document without even looking at it.

Postscript

Chip went on to become the CEO, but also the chief financial officer, chief operating officer, the vice president of human resources, director of procurement, manager of logistics, head of quality control, national sales manager and first, second, and third shift production supervisors, assembler, packer, and truck driver. He turned the company around in less than two years and made $2,500,000 on the sale.

Right way: Victory Enterprises

Background

While the previous case was based on one of my most colorful clients, Victory Enterprises is about one of the most impressive business leaders I have ever met. I was hired by Vic shortly after he became the president of a new division.

He brought me on his team to manage the purchasing and inventory control functions of his division. These were areas in which Vic had no experience; however, within a year, I had to step up my game because he had become my equal. I never met a quicker study; he was an absolute sponge.

This story is a good example of not only strength in many characteristics, but it clearly shows the power a person possesses when he has heightened business acumen. It was a great privilege to work with such a dynamic leader.

The Story

Vic was one of the most business savvy people I ever met. Not only was he extremely intelligent, but he appeared to have a sixth sense for business. He consistently made profitable business decisions throughout his entire career.

Part of Vic's success stemmed from his passion for learning. He saw every experience as an opportunity to gain knowledge and insight. When he was a salesman, he knew more about the products he sold than the engineers who designed them. He had a better understanding of the terms and conditions of their contracts than most of the company's lawyers who created them, and perhaps of even greater importance, he knew more about his competitors than they knew about themselves. Consequently, when it came to selling, Vic had no equal.

The first year he joined the company, Vic became the "Salesman of the Year." He held that title for the next fifteen years. His success was due to his business insight, product knowledge, and his strong ability to connect with people. He was so good at sales that he turned down countless promotions to management.

Finally, the CEO asked him to head up a new division and made him an offer he couldn't refuse. In one day, his title changed from "salesman" to "president."

Vic was one of those rare individuals who successfully transitioned from one career to another with ease. The focus, commitment, and business acumen that made him a great salesman served him well as the president of a multimillion-dollar organization.

The moment he took the position, he made it his mission to learn everything he could about the new products, the market, and his competition. He interviewed dozens of the brightest minds in the industry, read everything he could get his hands on, and even worked along side the technicians who assembled the products in the factory.

In a short time, Vic knew more about the "business" than anyone in the company. Unfortunately, at the same time, corporate profits of the parent company began to slip, and despite the fact that Vic's division was setting sales records, the board of directors demanded severe budget cuts. Vic tried to convince them that they were making a mistake, but they would not listen. They were more interested in short-term gains (i.e., their own bonuses) than long-term growth.

The cuts were so severe that they immediately began to have an effect on sales. He could not stand to see his competitors pass him, yet there was nothing he could do. Realizing that the board was not going to change their mind, he reorganized the division to compensate for the lack of funding and was about to turn things around when the board demanded a second round of cutbacks.

In order to meet their demands, Vic was forced to sell off his most profitable operations to his toughest competitors. He finally had enough and resigned. He sat on the sidelines and watched his former company self-destruct.

While on the bench, Vic put together a business plan so brilliant it rivaled the finest military strategies of all times. He used his knowledge of the industry to his own personal advantage. He began to promote himself as a subject matter expert. He wrote articles for professional journals, gave lectures at industrial conferences, and even hosted a roundtable discussion at an international conference in Zurich.

He ultimately used his popularity to launch a consulting practice. From the moment he opened the doors, he had every major company begging for his services. During his consulting engagements, Vic had unlimited access to all of his clients' critical information.

Within two years, Vic's prediction about his former company came true. The severe cutbacks eventually sent the division into a tailspin. Sales fell 60 percent, and the division was on the brink of bankruptcy when Vic launched his assault.

Although his consulting practice was successful and his speaking engagements were booked solid for over a year, he seized the opportunity to buy the failing division. By the time he made his offer, the board of directors almost paid him to take it off their hands.

Shockwaves were sent throughout the industry when word hit the street that Vic was going to be competing against the companies for which he had provided consulting services. The mere thought of him running his own company, after what he had learned about his competition, created fear in the minds of his competitors.

In an attempt to head off a potential disaster, the largest company in that industry made Vic an offer to prevent him from getting back into the game. They purchased the company from him before he had made the first payment on his loan from the original owners. No one knows the exact details, but it was rumored that he walked away with over $3,500,000 from the sale of the company.

In addition, in order to prevent Vic from joining any other firm or starting another company, the new owners paid him $250,000 per year, for the next ten years, to provide "advice and counsel" (corporate speak for "*stay home*").

Chapter 6

Case Studies on Sales Ability

Wrong way: The Universally Unusual Company

Background

A number of years ago, I was hired by the founder of the Universally Unusual Company (UUC) to create an inventory management system after he bought out a competitor. Although the company he acquired had a solid client base, it was losing money due to skyrocketing inventory costs caused by excessive waste, theft, and spoilage.

Jim (the owner) was confident he could turn the company around by introducing a new sales philosophy he had created. This is the tale of his unique approach.

The Story

Before starting his own company, Jim was the national sales manager for a regional office supply company. Although he claimed to have extensive sales experience, he was never actually a salesman. He was the CFO and inherited the sales department during a dramatic downsizing of his company.

It was ironic that he claimed sales expertise when, in fact, he had a negative opinion of the sales profession. Jim believed that most salespeople spent too much time trying to appease customers. He thought that salespeople should be product experts, and customers should heed their advice. His philosophy could be summed up in his favorite quote: *"The problem with most salespeople is that they listen too much."*

Jim wanted to start his own company so he could implement his unique sales model. Then, in a strange twist of fate, he got his wish when his employer eliminated his position after a second round of cutbacks. He used his severance package to buy a small janitorial supply company.

After the acquisition, Jim became a man on a mission. He set out to create a new business model that he believed would revolutionize the industry. The model was based on his belief that customers really have no idea what is best for them and that they needed to be directed. His mission was to educate his customers so they could make intelligent decisions.

Where the "unusual" part of the UUC name derives its meaning is from Jim's reaction when customers did not heed his advice. If they did not accept his recommendations, he would argue with them, or as he preferred to say, he would "educate the uninformed." For some strange reason, customers didn't like being lectured. After six months in business, Jim had generated less than $3,000 in sales.

Just when he was about to throw in the towel, he caught a huge break when a competitor was forced to sell his business due to legal problems. Jim was able to buy an established company for pennies on the dollar. He went from virtually zero sales to almost $100,000 overnight. Jim viewed the acquisition as a vindication of his methodology—despite the fact that he had not landed a single account on his own.

Jim hired me to develop an inventory management system for his new company, but when he sensed my disbelief in his sales approach, he made it his mission to convert me. He spent the next six months educating me on what he called his "Enlightenment Sales Model." The approach was based on two simple principles:

- ➢ Customers are clueless.
- ➢ Price is not important.

Unfortunately for Jim, his customers did not share these opinions. The following case best illustrates how Jim's revolutionary approach to sales worked out for him when dealing with one of his "clueless" customers.

The Case of the European Towel Dispensers

Jim represented over fifty different product lines, but his favorite was an unusual line of European bathroom fixtures. He especially liked the Euro 9000 hand towel dispensers. He believed they were the best product on the market. Unfortunately, customers showed no interest due to the cost and the practicality of their use. Not only were they expensive and difficult to install, but the towels were an unusual shape that cost three times more than the standard size. None of that mattered to Jim because he saw it as an opportunity to "enlighten."

One Friday morning, he received a rush order from one of the new customers he had inherited. Among the items requested was an order for twenty-five standard towel dispensers. Jim filled the order and personally delivered them to the customer. As he handed the buyer one of the European dispensers, he said, "Call your maintenance guy. I'll show him how to install it."

The buyer looked puzzled and said, "That's not what I ordered. I already told you that they are ugly and too expensive." Jim didn't say a word and went back to unloading the rest of the order. The customer assumed Jim would return later in the day with the units he had requested.

The next Monday I received a call from the buyer who was very upset because he had still not received his dispensers. I thought there was a mistake, so I asked Jim what he wanted to do. His face lit up as he said, "Watch and learn!" He ran back to the stockroom and retrieved twenty-five European dispensers and said: "Prepare to be enlightened!"

The buyer was waiting for us in front of the building. It was obvious that he was glad to see us, but his expression changed the minute he saw the dispensers. He blurted out, "What the hell is that?" Jim confidently responded, "The answer to all your problems."

The buyer blew up. "We've been over this before. I HATE them!" Jim acted as if he didn't hear a thing and launched into a product demonstration in the middle of the parking lot. The buyer threw his clipboard on the ground and stormed back to the building.

When I asked Jim what he was doing, he calmly replied: "I've got him right where I want him. Now he *has* to buy from me."

I was stunned, but Jim remained calm. He used the opportunity to "enlighten" me by explaining that he was using his "White Knight" sales strategy. He had never planned on giving the customer what he wanted. He assumed that once the customer was backed into a corner, he would be forced to accept Jim's preferred product.

I have seen the White Knight strategy work before; however, it is based on the simple fact that you actually have to "save the day." It doesn't work when you make customers angry by trying to sell them something they hate.

We stood in the parking lot for what seemed like an eternity. When we finally left, Jim said, "This guy is good, but he'll be back." He honestly believed that the buyer would beg us to return. Obviously that didn't happen.

Jim's business limped along for almost a year after that encounter. It ultimately was forced to close due to a lack of "enlightened" customers.

Right way: Selling Machine Unlimited

Background

Of all the successful people I have had the pleasure of knowing, the owner of Selling Machine Unlimited was one of the most inspirational. The most interesting part of Jane's story is that she had a limited education, no formal training, no mentors, and no one to support her—either emotionally or financially. She accomplished everything on her own by observing other successful people and emulating their behavior.

I was hired by Jane to develop an inventory tracking system. Her humble beginnings made her extremely cost conscious.

The Story

Jane seemed headed toward failure in almost every sense of the word. She had nothing going for her and everything going against her. Like so many young women, she was forced to leave high school to have a baby. Unfortunately, after less than a year of marriage, her husband left her and their daughter with no one to care for them.

Jane tried to balance minimum wage jobs and child care, but nothing worked. She finally moved in with her mother and found work as a night janitor in a large office complex. It was not a great job, but it allowed her to be with her daughter during the day.

One of the offices she cleaned was a medical supply company. Everyone liked Jane because she was so friendly and was always willing to go above and beyond her normal job requirements.

One night, Jane got a big break during a crisis at the firm. The day before a major proposal was due, the office was hit with an outbreak of the flu. All of the support staff called in sick, and the owner was trying to assemble the presentation by himself. Jane arrived at 8:00 p.m. to find the place in total chaos. She asked the owner if there was anything she could do, and he immediately put her to work. She was a quick study and did an outstanding job.

The owner himself became so sick that he had to leave shortly after getting Jane started. He planned to arrive early the next morning to complete the job. Jane stayed through the night and finished the project by herself. When the owner came in the next day, he was speechless.

Jane was rewarded for her good work by being fired from the maintenance firm. The other clients in the building complained that their offices were not cleaned, so they assumed she was goofing off. When the owner of the medical company heard about her termination, he immediately offered her a job. Not only did it pay better, they had a day care center for her daughter. Jane started out as the receptionist but rose rapidly through the ranks.

Jane was so grateful for the job that she worked hard to prove herself. She came in early, stayed late, and worked weekends. Within a few months, she was promoted to junior sales associate. She got all the accounts that no one else wanted, but her drive and ambition broke down doors that were previously closed. She was polite but persistent, and nothing could detract her from a sale.

When she lost a sale, she wanted to know why. She would respectfully ask her clients what she could have done better. It wasn't a trick; she genuinely wanted to know how to improve herself. Within five years, she was the number one sales person in the company.

The thing that made Jane different from the other sales people was that she made her customer's business "her" business. She had complete dossiers on all of her clients, their key managers, support personnel, and all gatekeepers.

She made a special point to cultivate close working relationships with all levels of management and went out of her way to develop friendships with anyone who came in contact with her products—from the people in the shipping department to quality control inspectors.

Jane never had any formal sales training—she learned everything through trial and error. As time passed, she developed her own style of dealing with customers. Rather than trying to convince customers to buy what she sold, she concentrated on listening to their problems.

Her goal was to be a source of knowledge for her customers. She wanted to be the first person they called when they had a problem, even if it didn't involve a product she sold.

Unfortunately, the job Jane enjoyed so much came to a sudden end. Her firm was acquired by a catalog supply company that conducted all of their business over the phone. All outside sales positions were eliminated and replaced with a call center in another country.

Although Jane was the top salesperson at her former company, no one would hire her because of her lack of education. She interviewed with dozens of companies, but no one would give her a chance without a degree. She finally came to the conclusion that, if she ever wanted to get back to doing what she loved, she would have to start her own company.

Although she was an outstanding sales person, she had no experience in working with bankers regarding commercial loans. Fortunately, her reputation for helping others paid off, and help came from an unlikely source.

When one of Jane's customers learned of her plight, she began making calls on her behalf. She persuaded a banker to give Jane a loan by signing a contract committing to buy three years worth of medical supplies from Jane's proposed company.

Jane approached ownership with the same dedication and commitment she made years early when she started in sales. She took courses, listened to CDs, and read everything she could get her hands on. She even formed a network of new small business owners and held regular meetings to share experience and advice.

As a business owner, she distinguished herself from the competition by becoming an incredible resource in all areas of business. If she didn't know an answer, she knew where to get it. She was proud of the fact that almost half of the inquiries she received were not related to anything she sold. She never complained; in fact, she felt honored to help.

The following story is an example of Jane's sales ability (with a touch of *business acumen* thrown in).

Jane's Christmas Story

Jane loved the holiday season both as a mother and a business professional. She spent the entire month of December visiting all of her clients to show her appreciation for their support. One year, one of her oldest and most loyal customers was on the verge of bankruptcy. Jane knew that they were not going to survive past the holidays, but rather than avoiding them, she went out of her way to make their last year special.

She made sure that everyone, from the president to the guys on the shipping dock, got a present. When she learned that the owner had to cancel the Christmas party due a lack of money, she jumped into action.

She dropped everything to create a memorable event. The night before the party, she convinced a security guard to let her in to decorate the soon-to-be-closed office. When the workers arrived the next morning, they were treated to a gala celebration that included great food, beverages, games, contests, and even a DJ.

At 5:00 p.m., when it was evident that no work was going to be done that day, Jane invited everyone back to her house for dessert. The party went into the wee hours of the morning, and a good time was had by all.

The point of the story is that, although Jane was genuinely moved by the plight of one of her customers, she had strong business reasons for her actions. I have to admit that as close as I was to the situation, I did not fully understand her brilliance.

Months later, she divulged her motives to me. Although she knew that the company was going out of business, she also realized that all of her contacts were in the prime of their working careers. The company was going away—not the people. She expressed her way of thinking best when she said, "I knew they (her contacts) were not going to be shipped to Siberia to shovel snow. They were all going to move on to new jobs at successful companies." Jane was right.

The thing that impressed me most about Jane was her ability to see an opportunity in the middle of a disastrous situation. As it turned out, her investment paid off big-time. There may be other examples, but I personally witnessed the following:

Jane's first payoff came from the owner of the company. Although his business had failed, he was back on his feet in a matter of months. He became the chief operating officer of a large hospital chain. Jane was the first person he called when he needed medical supplies.

The second payoff came from the purchasing agent at the company. Phyllis had such a great reputation that she had a new job within two weeks. She became the director of procurement for the largest medical center in the city, and guess who became her number one supplier?

The final benefit is probably the most memorable. Jane had great compassion for what she called the "invisible people," such as parking lot attendants, security guards, shipping clerks, receptionists, and secretaries. One of the people she went out of her way to please was the receptionist. Jane was concerned that Ruth, being older, would be without a job during the holidays. To remedy that situation, Jane created a job for her at her company.

Little did she know that Ruth did not need to work—she just liked to keep busy. Her son was the CEO of a major investment firm in New York. Ruth only went to work to stay active and to be around young people. During the holidays, at her son's place in the Hamptons, Ruth told her son about the lovely Christmas party that Jane put on when she learned Ruth's employer was going out of business.

Her son was so moved by the story that he flew out to personally meet Jane. Although his firm had no need for the medical supplies Jane sold, they financed many companies who did, and Ruth's son made sure they all knew about Jane. According to Jane's own estimates, her firm doubled in size within two years based on referrals from Ruth's son, alone.

Jane took thinking outside the box to a whole new level. She was not motivated by tricks or schemes; she honestly believed that becoming a valuable resource to her customers would insure her long-term success.

Jane gave me some of the best sales advice when she said, "I never tell my customers what I sell. I ask them what they need."

Chapter 7

Case Studies on Financial Intelligence

Wrong way: Plain Vanilla Software

Background

Plain Vanilla Software was an extremely conservative software company. Unfortunately, the term "conservative" is not viewed as a good thing in the software industry. The problem was that their products were perceived as being stodgy by some clients. The truth however, was that their software was simply too complex for many customers to understand.

The board of directors placed the blame for the image problem on the CEO. Although he had turned a disorganized start-up company into a multimillion-dollar operation, and had sustained a ten percent growth per year for almost twenty years, he was replaced with a fresh face from outside of the industry to turn things around.

Before their demise, I was hired by the vice president of sales to develop a training program to demystify their products, so that customers could better understand, and take advantage of the many features and benefits of their powerful software. While there, I witnessed firsthand the complete destruction of a strong and viable company.

The Story

A new CEO was brought in from the outside to breathe life into the company. The board was impressed with Chris's dynamic personality and strong sense of self-confidence. They gave him their full support and a free hand to do whatever he thought necessary to take the company to the next level.

Although he could be charming, Chris was very opinionated and had, what polite people call, a "healthy" ego. He approached business with two basic assumptions: The first was that everything done before he arrived was wrong; and second, most people could not appreciate his insight because they lacked his vision. I'm not being sarcastic; his exact quote to his management team at his first staff meeting was: "I don't expect most of you to understand what I'm doing, because few people have my special gifts."

Before he set foot in the building, Chris already knew exactly what was wrong with the company. Of all of the pressing issues facing the organization, Chris decided that the first thing that had to be addressed was the name of the company.

He commissioned a high-profile agency to create a new company name and logo. The agency invented a mysterious Swiss sounding name that was difficult to pronounce and hard to spell. Chris believed that it created an aura of mystery and intrigue. The $250,000 spent on the consultant was just the tip of the iceberg; everything from signage to business cards had to be changed.

His next priority was the annual technology workshop, which had been a tradition since the inception of the company. The previous CEO viewed the workshops as an outstanding opportunity to work closely with their clients to truly understand their needs.

Technicians from their major customers came from across the country to work with the best software designers in the company to solve problems and create new products. Over the years, the workshop produced hundreds of brilliant ideas.

The workshop had been a modest affair in which each attendee paid his own way. The conference room served as a computer lab, dining room, kitchen, and at times, a dorm room. The company provided pizza, soda, and chocolate chip cookies. The attendees were serious "techies" who came to exchange ideas.

Unfortunately, Chris did not like anything about the event. He was appalled to learn that there were no guest speakers, entertainment, or fun activities. He described it as a "nerd fest."

He felt the conference should have a much more strategic, or high-level, focus. He was convinced that they needed to interact with a higher caliber of clientele, so he only invited directors and vice presidents.

He also changed the event from a "workshop" to an "Executive Roundtable" and held it at a resort near Lake Tahoe, thousands of miles from their offices. To insure a large turnout, he picked up the tab for all participants, including airfare, hotels, meals, and entertainment.

The event began on Sunday with a golf outing at a private country club, followed by a reception at a popular art gallery. Monday featured a nationally recognized motivational speaker, followed by workshops on improving interpersonal skills, such as communications, decision making, and the benefits of deep breathing through meditation (*I'm not making this up*).

On Tuesday, Chris gave a presentation in the grand ballroom in which he revealed his vision of the future (which incidentally had nothing to do with software). His speech was followed by a lavish lunch and an afternoon of "team building exercises," such as rappelling off a fake plastic mountain next to the tennis courts.

Wednesday culminated with a roundtable discussion on what customers really wanted. Normally this would have been valuable if anyone remotely knowledgeable about the product was in attendance. Unfortunately all of the participants were four or five levels removed from programmers. The first conference produced the following ground-breaking suggestions to improve their software:

1. Make it more powerful.
2. Lower the price.

Astonishing!

After the roundtable, Chris turned his attention to the operational side of the business. When he asked his staff what they needed most, the number one answer was laptop computers. Under the previous administration, although everyone had a PC at their desk, laptops were regarded as true luxuries and only field technicians received them. In response to this request, every staff member was given a powerful new laptop.

The company ended up owning 285 computers for their 125 employees. An entire storeroom was filled with over a hundred perfectly good desktop computers that were never used again.

Chris then focused his attention on his most ambitious project—the facility upgrade. The first thing to go was the old warehouse location. Although it was extremely functional, he thought it was too cliché, so he moved the entire company to the top floor of one of the nicest high-rises in the city.

Before taking possession of the new facility, Chris hired a premier design firm to do a complete makeover. Modest $100 workstation chairs were replaced with $3,500 ergonomic "seating experiences," and grey fabric acoustical cubical panels were replaced with glass "design segments." But the most unusual change was the lobby. Imported leather sofas and a large flat screen TV were added, along with a waterfall to create "white noise."

What made this "improvement" so unusual was that the company never had visitors. They produced mainframe software that ran on their customers' computers. If there was a problem, the engineers flew to the client's location. In the twenty years the company had been in business, they never had a single customer visit their facility, other than the annual workshop participants.

HR was the last area of opportunity for Chris. While the previous administration held a hard line on staffing, Chris opened the doors. Anything that fell under the umbrella of "new" or "innovative" interested him. As a result, twenty new jobs were created. Positions, such as a receptionist for a lobby that never had guests, were added to the payroll.

His final staff addition raised the eyebrows of even his staunchest supporters. Chris viewed himself as a visionary, so in order to capture his legacy; he created a position called *director of change management*. It was a full-time job with a six-figure salary.

He hired a professional writer from an advertising agency. Her primary responsibility was to capture Chris's insight and create suitable formats for others to enjoy his teachings. She produced monthly newsletters, a year end "State of the Vision" report and published copies of Chris's speeches.

As a result of Chris's changes, the board got their wish; he did make a huge impact on the bottom line of the company— unfortunately, it wasn't the impact they wanted. Before Chris was handed control of this strong and viable company, annual sales exceeded $60 million, and the stock was at $42.00 per share, with no debt, and a financial cushion over $10 million in cash and other assets.

Within two years of his arrival, sales dropped to $35 million, their stock had diminished in value to less than $1.00 a share, the cash reserves were completely gone, and they had incurred $6,000,000 of debt.

The straw that broke the camel's back took place when the company attempted to upgrade their product. Upgrades are the lifeblood of the software industry—not only do they keep the products fresh and alive, but they are extremely profitable.

Chris's spending spree left the company on the verge of bankruptcy. In addition to squandering all of their liquid assets, he damaged their credit rating so badly they were unable to raise a modest $100,000, of the $1,000,000 needed, for the upgrade.

When the board finally learned how bad things were, they demanded his resignation. A new CEO was brought in to clean house. Unfortunately, he was faced with the daunting task of trying to turn around a company that had declining sales, obsolete products, no cash reserves, massive debt, outrageously high operating costs, and a terrible credit rating.

As good as he was, he couldn't put off the inevitable, and within six months, the company was out of business. Twenty years of strong financial control were destroyed in less than two years of reckless and unnecessary spending.

Right way: Tight Ship Incorporated

Background

Tight Ship Incorporated (TSI) was the complete opposite of Plain Vanilla Software. TSI started out as a simple company that produced plastic bottle caps for the soft drink industry. Two brothers began the company in a converted gas station. As time passed, they diversified their product line to include everything from children's toys to products for the Defense Department.

They ran their operations completely debt free for over twenty years by keeping a close eye on all expenditures. I was hired to develop a system to track their production costs. The brothers loved statistics and wanted to know the exact financial position of their company at all times.

The Story

As TSI grew and acquired new companies, they consolidated all of their manufacturing and administration operations into one facility. The operation gave new meaning to the term "lean." There were no secretaries or administrative assistants. Everyone answered their own phone, made their own copies, and took turns making coffee. No one had to water the plants because there were none. The only extravagance was a kitchenette with a refrigerator and a microwave.

Every phone in the office had a bright red label that said, "NO PERSONAL CALLS." The brothers bought special PCs that did not have external drives or Internet access; the sealed units prevented employees from downloading games or copying company secrets.

There was no maintenance or janitorial staff. Everyone was responsible for his or her own area, including taking out the garbage. If anything needed to be fixed, the owners usually did it. There were no luxurious offices or conference rooms, and although the furniture was of sound quality, everything was purchased at factory liquidation sales.

Business travel was conducted by car and reimbursed at standard IRS rates. Employees shared hotel rooms and were given a flat $25.00 per diem, no matter what city was visited. All company entertaining was done pot luck, with employees providing the food and drink. The owners supplied the paper plates and plastic utensils.

The brothers only spent money on two things—customers and the factory.

Anything that a customer needed was provided. If a client needed help installing a product, a technician would be sent, free of charge. If they received a defective part, one of the owners would personally deliver the replacement.

The factory earned the same consideration. If a new tool was needed to improve quality or lower costs, it was provided. If an operator needed special training, he or she got it. If the shipping department needed a new forklift, they got it. The factory wasn't glamorous, but it had the best equipment in the industry. The bottom line was that the owners only spent money when there was a return on their investment.

One of the other keys to the brothers' success was that they never let their success go to their heads. Even during the best of times, when they were making record-setting profits, they didn't change their method of operation. They ran as lean in the good times as they did in the bad.

Although some employees complain that TSI is not the most fun place to work, everyone respects the owners for what they have accomplished. They have never missed a payroll, and no one has ever been laid off. Although the compensation is not extravagant, it is fair.

Most importantly, the owners lead by example. They are the first to arrive and the last to leave. They never take long lunches or miss time to go golfing. Although they are very wealthy, they never flaunt it. None have private offices, company cars, or generous expense accounts. The owners pay their own way and never take company assets for personal use.

The brothers are reaping the benefits of their financial intelligence. While the rest of the economy began a downturn in 2006, their sales actually increased because many of their competitors were forced out of business. In an industry that suffered its worst sales in fifty years, 2007 was one of their best.

They recently celebrated their twenty-fifth anniversary. During that period, they have never posted a loss and managed to increase sales an average of 8–12 percent per year. They have always been debt free and own over $12 million in property and other assets.

The eldest brother stated their philosophy best when he said, "The company exists for one and only one reason—to generate enough profit to provide comfortable livings for the owners, the employees, and their families."

Chapter 8

Case Studies on Political Intelligence

Wrong way: "That's Not Fair!"

Background

Greg came from a broken home and at an early age found himself in serious trouble with the law. Judged guilty of crimes that should have sent him to a juvenile detention center until the age of eighteen, a compassionate judge sent him to a special technical school for troubled teenagers rather than prison.

It was during this confinement that Greg's life was transformed from a troubled teen to a young man filled with hope and purpose. In addition to teaching him a trade as a mechanical engineer, the institution provided a strong background in religion and moral counseling.

Unfortunately, like some people who overcome adversity, Greg began to overcompensate. As time passed he developed very strong beliefs about what he perceived to be "proper" personal behavior. Those beliefs eventually spilled over to his business life.

Upon graduation, Greg landed a good job as a mechanic in a large factory but was unable to advance due his lack of a formal education. He bounced from job to job until he decided to strike out on his own. I met Greg shortly after he had received a loan from the Small Business Administration to create a company to manufacture specialty parts for the automotive industry.

I was hired to develop a system to monitor production costs and to make recommendations for reducing operating expenses.

The Story

Greg was a genius in solving mechanical problems. He could evaluate difficult situations and design solutions better than anyone in the business. Although he could create brilliant products, he failed to understand the importance of cultivating business relationships.

Because of his strong moral beliefs about what he considered proper business conduct, Greg never sought to interact with his clients on a personal level. In order to prevent any hint of impropriety, he avoided any unnecessary client contact. He believed that all business transactions should be conducted at "arm's length" and that there should be no mingling between the parties.

As time passed, Greg's beliefs became more extreme. As a result, he saw improprieties everywhere—even in the most innocent behaviors, such as a buyer and salesperson conversing over a cup of coffee.

He became obsessed with identifying improprieties and felt it was his duty to make everyone aware of his observations. He initiated a letter writing campaign to the senior management of all of his potential customers alerting them of his concerns about unethical business practices. In a short time, Greg gained a reputation for being a troublemaker.

He firmly believed that all he had to do was produce the right product, at the right price, and that every company should immediately award him their business. He was convinced that it was just a matter of time before his potential customers would come to their senses and see that he was right. He honestly expected to receive calls from every CEO he contacted, thanking him for his honesty and awarding him all of their business. Unfortunately that never happened.

The sad part of this story was that no one ever asked him to do anything wrong. Nobody expected to be wined and dined or receive any form of gratuities. All his buyers wanted were good products at good prices.

Final Thoughts

This case has an ironic twist. Greg's obsession with fairness prevented him from realizing the special gifts that he had already been given. As a legally classified "small and disadvantaged" owner, he received a low-interest business loan, training assistance, and was eligible to participate in multiple federally funded programs.

It's ironic to note that his company actually enjoyed a special status. City, state and local governments had special "set aside" programs that mandated that corporations give companies like his preferential treatment over "non-disadvantaged" companies.

All of Greg's problems could have been prevented had he learned the first rule of preschool: "Play nice in the sandbox."

Right way: A True Entrepreneur

Background

Eric had no business experience prior to starting his own company. All he had were incredible powers of observation, the ability to connect with people, and an uncanny sense of political insight.

Eric had a brilliant military career until, as he put it, "Peace broke out all over the world." He loved the army and never planned on leaving, but budget cuts in the 1980s forced him and thousands of his peers out.

To make matters even worse, his dedication to the service cost him his marriage. The years of relocations had taken its toll, and his wife left him during his final tour of duty in South Korea. In one year, Eric lost his career and his marriage

This is his story.

The Story

Eric had traveled all over the world during his twenty years in the service, but none of his assignments were as foreign to him as returning to civilian life. He had been a soldier more than half of his life, having gone directly from high school into boot camp.

The world had changed so much in the time he was gone that he had a hard time adjusting. Despite his long and distinguished career, he had nothing to show for it. He always lived on base and never owned a house. With four children, his modest military pay did not go far. His wife got all of their furniture in the divorce, and other than his pension, he had no other financial resources.

A friend offered him a place to stay in Chicago, so he packed all of his possessions into a duffle bag and boarded a bus. Upon his arrival, he was dealt another blow when his friend rescinded his offer due to marital problems of his own. Eric found himself homeless, broke, and in a strange city. With nowhere to go, he turned to the only place he knew: the army. Fortunately, a local base offered him temporary shelter.

Eric's first priority was to find a job, but his skills as a munitions expert were not in demand in the private sector. His only job before the army was frying hamburgers. He was almost forty years old, and had no marketable skills.

Having never interviewed for a job, Eric had no idea where to begin. One day, while driving around a large industrial complex, a help wanted sign for "millwrights" caught his attention. Although he had no idea what millwrights did, he decided to apply anyway.

Since most millwrights don't wear three-piece suits on interviews, the receptionist didn't think he was applying for a job in the factory, so she assumed he was there for the "big meeting." She handed him a large envelope and directed him to the conference room, which was packed with people listening to a presentation. Eric had no idea what was happening, but something told him to play along.

The person leading the meeting was the director of purchasing. He started by saying, "I have a lot to cover in a short amount of time. Hold all your questions until the end. We will break up into smaller groups, and you'll work directly with my buyers."

The director's presentation focused on a new product being developed by the company. The audience consisted of salesmen from competing firms vying for contracts to manufacture the major components. When the presentation was over, the audience disbanded into smaller groups around the corporate buyers. It was total chaos; everyone was talking at the same time. Eric drifted from conversation to conversation trying to learn as much as he could.

The discussions went on for hours. At the end of the day, Eric was the last one left. He was sitting alone in the conference room reviewing some blueprints when the director of purchasing walked past. When he saw Eric, he said, "Well, this is a first, a salesman working overtime!"

Eric had no idea what he meant, but he inferred from the tone of his voice that salesmen were not held in the highest regard. When he introduced himself, the director noticed his army ring and said, "Where were you stationed?" Eric said, "You mean where *wasn't* I stationed?" Both men laughed, and the director said, "Yeah, you don't look like a salesman. Follow me."

The director took him back to his office and poured two glasses of bourbon. They swapped war stories until the director said, "Do you like steak?" They adjourned to a local restaurant and spent the rest of the evening telling army stories. The director loved to talk, and Eric was more than willing to accommodate him. Every word he spoke divulged something about himself or his company.

At the end of dinner, Eric was awarded something for which he wasn't prepared. Although the director had invited *him* to dinner, Eric was expected to pick up the tab. That presented a real problem since he only had $23.58 cents to his name, and the bill was almost $100.

When the check came, the director stood up, thanked him for the great time, and left. He was alone in the restaurant with a check that was four times more than he had in his wallet. Eric thought about running, but his ethics were too strong, so he decided to improvise.

He complemented the waitress on her outstanding service and gave her a $20.00 tip. He asked to speak to the manager because he wanted to tell him how much he loved the restaurant.

The manager was delighted with the praises and said, "Do you work with Mr. Thomas (the director)?" Eric replied, "I'll be doing lots of work with him the future, and I would love to make your restaurant my base of operations. How do I set up an account?"

Without hesitation, the manager took the check and tucked it into his pocket and said, "Consider it done." Eric's luck had finally started to turn.

He returned to the barracks and stayed up most of the night trying to process everything that had just happened. He spent the next day learning as much as he could about the project. Despite his best efforts, there was too much information. The bid package contained over five hundred components that needed pricing. Fortunately there was an incredible engineering department on base, and Eric convinced them to help him out.

He also needed to understand more about the business side of his new life. He learned that many manufacturing companies used outside people called "sales reps" and paid them commissions on what they sold. It was a good deal for the companies because they did not have to pay anything unless the rep sold something. It was also a good deal for the sales person because they could represent multiple companies.

The next day Eric called his new friend, the director, and invited him to lunch. It was a great meeting. Eric gained incredible insight when the director said, "Don't kill yourself chasing all the small crap. Leave that for the slugs—just focus on the big stuff." Eric thought about that comment for a moment and asked, "What's most important for you?"

The director let down his guard and told him everything he needed to know including how much he was willing to pay. The conversation ended with:

> Director: "Can you get me actuators?"
> Eric: "Yes I can."
> Director: "Great, you will be a hero around here. We can't find any worth a damn. We are paying $37.80, and they are total crap. If you could find me good ones, I'd be willing to pay $50.00 each."

Eric had one question, but he didn't dare ask. His only question was, "What is an *actuator*?"

As soon as the meeting was over, Eric raced back to the base to meet the chief engineering officer. Not only did he know everything about actuators, he also knew the best manufacturers in the country. By the time Eric left, he was an expert as well.

But finding a manufacturer qualified to produce the actuator Eric needed was more difficult than he anticipated. He interviewed over a dozen companies, and none could meet his customer's tight specifications. He needed a special source. He finally went to the last company on the list. The only reason they were not ranked higher was because they had just lost a major military contract due to budget cutbacks, and their future was uncertain.

They were located in the middle of nowhere. Eric drove five hours to meet them, but it was worth the trip. Not only did their engineers know exactly what he needed, they laughed when he asked if they could meet his customer's tight specifications. One engineer joked, "We throw out better stuff!"

Eric was afraid that their high quality would make them too expensive. He became very concerned when the manager said, "Your client is looking for very sophisticated actuators." Eric held his breath—the manager continued, "Building them is no problem, but we will have to charge you $19.95 each."

Eric's pulse began to race. He couldn't calculate the potential, but he knew it was good. He took a deep breath and thanked them for their time. His legs could barely support his weight as he walked back to the car. The contract was for ten thousand units.

At the time Eric closed the deal, he literally did not have enough money to buy gas to drive back to the manufacturer to deliver the contract in person. That single order, however, earned him over $200,000 (in 1987). He never had to worry about gas money again.

Everyone won! His customer received a great product that solved all of their quality problems, the manufacturer was saved from bankruptcy, and Eric was able to move out of the barracks—but he wasn't finished. He came to the conclusion that his customer could not possibly be the only company in the country that needed precision actuators, and he was right.

He used his first commission check to buy a car and set out on the road to pursue other customers. Within two years, he was making over $500,000 a year on actuators alone. He went on to represent over one hundred different product lines and amassed a substantial fortune.

Eric was a true entrepreneur.

Chapter 9

Case Studies on Focus

Wrong way: The Dream Come True Company

Background

How many people would jump at the chance to receive a grant, not a loan, large enough to start a new business? Although an opportunity like that doesn't come along often, that is exactly what happened to Ryan.

Not only was the grant large enough to start a company, it also provided a generous monthly income to relieve Ryan of the pressures of supporting his family. It was truly a dream come true.

Ryan knew what hard work was all about, so he deeply appreciated the opportunity. Raised in poverty, he struggled for over ten years to earn a college degree while juggling two jobs and starting his family. He graduate with honors and was awarded a grant from the foundation of a wealthy philanthropist.

The award was based upon a brilliant term paper Ryan had written for a course on small business development. His business plan was so brilliant that the board awarded him the highest monetary grant in the history of the foundation.

I was hired by the foundation to develop an inventory management program to keep operating costs to a minimum. Ryan had it all: financial backing and professional guidance.

The Story

The business plan, approved by the foundation, was for the creation of a small, light-duty assembly factory to produce surgical supply kits for hospitals. The process was simple—Ryan would purchase various surgical tools according to hospital specifications, sterilize them, and vacuum seal them into kits.

Ryan had three major tasks to complete in order to launch his business. First, he had to negotiate contracts for the surgical tools. Second, he had to purchase equipment to sterilize the products, and third, he had to hire staff to assemble the kits.

Things went well at first; however, progress began to decline when he was unable to negotiate acceptable prices on the main product—scalpels. For all of his intelligence, Ryan made a critical mistake in overestimating his purchasing power. He failed to take into account his lack of leverage due to the size of his company.

For example, he thought that buying twenty-five thousand scalpels a year was a large amount, but what he did not realize was that some of his competitors used that many in a day. He made the same mistake on the price of the sterilizers. He thought suppliers would give him their best price because he was buying two units; not realizing that the big companies had hundreds of them.

Being confronted with these obstacles was not an issue for Ryan. He was more than capable of critically analyzing even the most complex problems. Unfortunately, it was this strength that caused him to fail. His ability to visualize multiple solutions to complex problems caused him to get distracted from his original goals and objectives. Although his research was brilliant, it caused him to lose focus.

The following are two examples of his loss of focus:

Obstacle #1 Surgical Instruments

Since he could not negotiate prices that would allow him to be profitable, Ryan began analyzing the possibility of producing his own instruments. For example, rather than buying finished scalpels, he investigated what it would cost to purchase surgical grade steel, form it into the proper shapes, and sharpen them to medical grade specifications.

This was no easy task; he was not stamping out EXIT signs for freeways.

Obstacle #2 Capital Equipment

Ryan acquired the specifications for sterilizers and came to the conclusion that they were not too complicated. He spent weeks studying ways of making his own. Again, he underestimated the task, assuming that all that all he had to do was to accumulate the necessary components and hire someone to put them together. He failed to realize that they were potentially hazardous machines that had to be certified by federal safety inspectors.

Ryan's resolve was never in doubt. He met every obstacle head-on and fought his way through every problem. Unfortunately, the massive amount of analytical work he was conducting was robbing him of his most precious asset: time. Rather than focusing on his original goal of assembling simple surgical kits, he was consumed with analyzing multiple manufacturing alternatives.

When he presented his first progress report to the foundation at the three-month milestone, they expressed strong concern about his lack of progress. According to the original agreement, he was supposed to have all of his equipment in place and he should have been conducting test runs on his process as required by medical regulatory agencies. Instead, he had not purchased a single piece of equipment, signed any material contracts, or hired his first employee.

Although the committee complemented him on the quality of his research on vertical integration, they strongly encouraged him to return to his original plan and reminded him of the January 1 date he had committed to for being fully operational—a date that was just three months away.

Ryan reluctantly agreed, but immediately changed his mind when he returned to his office. He was not attempting to deceive the board; he was convinced that he could resolve his problems by controlling all aspects of the manufacturing process. He was certain that once the foundation saw his new research, they would be so impressed that he would be granted additional time to develop his new business model.

As good as his plans looked on paper, they fell apart in application. However, rather than shifting his focus toward fulfilling his obligations to the foundation, Ryan's research actually increased. It seemed that every new problem uncovered dozens of other "opportunities"; all of which evolved into other problems. Again, instead of giving up, Ryan increased his analytical efforts.

For example, in the area of producing his own scalpels, he was faced with a dozen different alternatives. He spent weeks trying to resolve his economies-of-scale problems. In order for Ryan to justify the purchase of the expensive manufacturing equipment, he needed to produce a minimum of five hundred thousand scalpels a year. Since his own company only required twenty-five thousand, he attempted to find other sources that could use his excess capacity (475,000 units).

He failed to realize that not only was the market flooded with qualified suppliers, but that most of his potential customers did not like the idea of buying from an unproven start-up company. Once again, rather than giving up, he dug in and investigated the potential of selling internationally, which brought on its own set of complex issues.

This is just one of dozens of options he was considering.

The bottom line is that, although his intentions were pure, all of Ryan's research was taking him away from his original plans. His desire for perfection robbed him of his focus on creating the company he had so brilliantly described in his college thesis.

At the foundation meeting in January, the board said that they were impressed with his research but terminated the grant due to his failure to meet the terms of the original business plan.

A senior member of the foundation said it best in his summation, "I'd rather have a 50 percent solution today, than a perfect one in two years."

Final Thoughts

What so many entrepreneurs fail to understand is that the business world rewards "closure." Income generation is essential to sustaining the life of a company. The only way to generate income is through the sale of products.

Right way: Serious Walt

Background

A number of years ago I was hired by an executive recruiting firm in Southern California to develop a performance management program to track the profitability of their sales force. While there, I met a truly unique person named Walt.

The Story

"Unique" is not the word most people used to describe Walt. Other expressions like *rude* and *obnoxious* were far more common. I didn't care much for Walt at first. He was one of the most condescending and aloof people I had ever met, which made me curious about his track record in sales. Not only was he the leading salesperson, but he outperformed the next four salespeople combined.

The quality that stuck me most about Walt was his antisocial behavior. He appeared to have no personality; however, after a week on the job, it became clear to me that there were two "Walts." There was "Inside Walt," the one I've been describing, and "Outside Walt," the world-class sales professional.

My impression that he was rude was based on the fact that he never socialized with anyone in the office; in fact, he rarely came out of his office. I had always been taught that being a team player was critical to success, but what I failed to realize, and what Walt understood perfectly, was that *his* business was not a team sport. From a strictly professional perspective, he had nothing in common with anyone else at the company.

Walt was not a bad person who stole candy off other people's desks or poured hot sauce in the coffee pot. He simply did not go out of his way to be nice. Everyone knew not to ask him to buy Girl Scout cookies or sign get-well cards. He never contributed to birthday parties, baby showers, or holiday celebrations. All he did was work.

Although he was part of a large recruiting agency, he had a very unique relationship with the original owners. He was a true independent contractor, and as such he provided his own furniture, phone system, computers, software, printers, scanners, copiers, fax machines, and even a separate customer database. The only thing he had in common with the other employees was the roof over their heads.

Walt joined the firm ten years earlier, after he lost his job as a VP of engineering when the company for which he worked went out of business. He had a difficult time finding work because all potential employers thought he was overqualified. Finally, a small (at the time) employment agency gave him a chance.

He was originally hired as a recruiter for secretarial help. As it turned out, he was terrible at this type of work and was ultimately fired. Not being one to give up, Walt approached the owner of the agency with a plan. Since his background was of a technical nature, he asked to develop a market exclusively for mechanical engineers, but the owner hated the idea and turned him down.

Convinced his idea had merit, Walt approached the owner again with another idea—Walt would work for "free." He promised to pay all of his own expenses. In essence, Walt would be an independent contractor with no cost to the owner whatsoever. Walt sealed the deal by agreeing to pay the company an additional 3 percent over the standard recruiting commission.

Walt's business took off immediately, and over the next ten years he paid the owner over $500,000 in commissions.

Eventually, the company was passed down to the next generation. As often happens when the "kids" take over, the new owners had no appreciation for the unique relationship that Walt had with their parents, nor did they understand the financial contributions he brought to the table. In an attempt to save some money, and increase their own personal wealth, they attempted to convert Walt from an independent business operator to a full time employee (at a greatly reduced pay level).

Walt was a seasoned professional and wanted no part of their plan. Knowing his value in the market, he tendered his resignation. He was calling his customers while he was packing his personal effects and closed his first deal while waiting for the moving van to pick up his furniture. Not only did he not lose a single client in the transition, his profits increased by eliminating the commissions he paid to the original owners.

The key to Walt's success was simple; Walt went to work, to work. He never made personal calls, played solitaire on his computer, or hung around the break room talking about who was dating whom or who he thought would win the big game. His ability to focus on business allowed him to block out all forms of distractions.

When he was engaged with a client, nothing else mattered. He focused on every word they said and, as a result, always knew exactly what his customers needed. His customers loved him because they felt they were his number one priority—and they were right.

Walt's philosophy about work is best summarized by his answer to my question as to why he never socialized in the office. He said, "Customers buy from me—co-workers don't."

Final Thoughts

Although I never understood why Walt could not have been a little nicer to the people around him, I was impressed with his results. His performance caused me to reevaluate the nonproductive activities that rob all companies of millions of dollars of profits a year.

Walt ran his business free of *all* forms of distractions. Although he was not the nicest person in the world, he delivered outstanding service and was extremely profitable, but most importantly, his customers *loved* him.

Chapter 10

Case Studies on Commitment

Wrong way: Joe Incorporated

Background

Joe was one of those rare people you think you know, but after a short time, you discover that you were completely wrong. Joe had all the right stuff; he was tall and handsome, with perfect hair, teeth, and eyes. He was a sharp dresser and had a charming personality.

If all that wasn't enough, he was a gifted speaker and had published two books on business development. Not only did he enjoy a brilliant career at one of the most successful consulting agencies in the country, he also sat on the advisory boards of numerous small companies and charitable organizations.

When he started his own company, people lined up to be a part of the action. I was fortunate enough to be hired to develop a training program. He wanted me to teach his people how to become professional consultants skilled in developing project plans, conducting critical-path analysis exercises, and identifying cost-savings opportunities for their clients.

The Story

Joe used his reputation to convince a group of investors to finance his new company. The interesting part was that the investors actually had no idea what they were investing in because Joe never clearly stated the mission of his company. Despite his ambiguity, Joe was able to raise over $2,000,000. In the final analysis, the investors were really just investing in Joe.

I was impressed with Joe until I worked with him for about a month. I realized that his powerful personality was what attracted people to him. You could not help but like him. He was charismatic, and his enthusiasm was contagious.

There was one problem however; Joe was like the proverbial mountain lake that is two miles across and two inches deep. He was, by his own admission, a "blue-sky guy." He loved coming up with ideas, but hated the details required to implement them.

Since he was fortunate enough to have ample funding, he was able to hire the necessary staff to carry out his plans. He viewed his role as president to be a "visionary." Unfortunately, most of his "visions" were abstract concepts that were not given much real thought. Although many were thought-provoking, few had real commercial value. The following are some of his more memorable creations:

> Innovation through elimination.
> Revolutionize decision making by accentuating creativity.
> Create innovation in profitability through focus on action over reaction.

Joe's fatal flaw was not readily apparent, because he was good at many other things. His charming personality made him a natural leader. A quick wit and sharp sense of humor made him an outstanding sales person. As a brilliant public speaker he could get people excited about his ideas; however, he lacked one key ingredient necessary for success—the commitment necessary to fight through adversity in order to attain success.

Although he was initially excited about all of his programs, he would quickly change course when he met any form of resistance. This was not the case of a person who hated confrontation; Joe could hold his own in an argument. His problem was that he felt that he had so many good ideas floating around in his head that he could not afford to waste too much time on anything that was not an immediate success.

His lack of commitment went to the core of the existence of his company. Joe's initial vision was to create a "revolutionary" consulting practice. He dedicated 100 percent of his time the first six months to selling his services. He was completely surprised when his first three prospects turned him down, so he put the practice on hold and changed to software development, claiming that the market was not ready for his vision of consulting.

He then threw all of his time and resources into creating an "evolutionary" software program. Unfortunately, his software received the same results as his consulting—no takers. After only three sales attempts, he assumed that the market was not ready for his software, so he returned to consulting. He continued this seesaw approach for the next two years.

It must be noted that these were not halfhearted attempts. Joe went full-out and gave each sales call 100 percent of his attention. His enthusiasm was never in doubt; it was his lack of commitment that was the problem.

Joe eventually ran out of money and was forced to liquidate everything.

Final Thoughts

This case is especially tragic because Joe was really on to something. All of the consultants he hired used the materials and training they had received at his company and went on to great careers with other organizations.

Although Joe never sold a single copy of his software, the person who bought the rights made a killing. A bright young entrepreneur purchased all of the programs for $25,000 and in less than a year sold them to a large software company for $1,250,000. The interesting part was that he did not change a single thing; he just went "door-to-door" until he found the right fit at the right company.

Not only does this case demonstrate the fatal flaw of lack of commitment, but it also proves one of the other lessons—personal success while working in a large company does not guarantee success as a business owner.

In a corporate environment, Joe had to follow the directives of his management. He was assigned projects that he was expected to complete and was not given the option to abandon them when he lost interest.

As the president of his own company, he could pick and choose whatever projects he liked. Joe did not fail because he was lazy or had bad products; he failed because he lacked the commitment to stick with programs long enough for them to succeed.

Right way: The King of Commitment

Background

I met Terry under unusual circumstances; in fact, we were never formally introduced. As I recall, our first meeting was more like running to catch a train that was screaming through a station. It took everything I had to catch up and hold on.

Before I go any further, I need to provide some background on the main character. Terry began his career as a teenager when he was forced to leave school to help support his family after the sudden passing of his father. He lied about his age and was hired to run a punch press in a local factory in Michigan.

He took the hardest jobs because they paid the most, and he volunteered for as much overtime as he could get. Management loved him because of his work ethic, and everyone in the factory liked him because he was always willing to help anyone in need. By the time he turned forty, he had been with the company for twenty-five years.

The Story - Part I: Conflict

I had just been hired as a purchasing agent for a large manufacturing company that was launching a new product. My first day on the job, I was pulled out of the new employee orientation program to attend a meeting that had been in progress for five hours. I took a seat in the back of a packed conference room and saw what looked like a press conference—or a firing squad.

Dozens of people from my company were shouting questions at the lone figure standing at the front of the room. Terry no sooner finished answering one question when two to three more were fired in his direction. Clearly, there was a problem, and everyone in the room held him responsible for solving it.

It turned out that *our* inspection department accidentally destroyed all of the samples his company had made for our new product line. Although it was our fault, we still held his company responsible for the replacements. We had less than two months to complete our finished products or risk losing millions of dollars of governmental contracts.

The normal timeframe for manufacturing his parts was fourteen to sixteen weeks, but Terry was given only seven weeks to perform. To make matters worse, our company mandated that he use raw materials that were only available in Japan. Their lead-time alone to manufacture and ship the material to the United States was six weeks, which left Terry's company less than seven days to build and deliver their finished products.

Terry stood in front of the hostile audience and continued to field questions for two more hours. The meeting finally came to an end when our VP of operations stated that the $6,000,000 contract enjoyed by Terry's company would be cancelled if he failed to make our deadline. There was no ambiguity in his message; he was dead serious.

New to the company, I could only sit and watch this drama unfold. What impressed me the most was that Terry's composure never changed throughout the entire ordeal. He remained calm and never lost control. When the meeting was over, he turned his attention to me because I was the buyer assigned to his account.

He spent the next hour explaining the complete manufacturing process. I was both depressed and impressed. I was depressed by the magnitude of our problem, but also impressed by Terry's grasp on the situation. Although I had only known him for a few hours, I felt confident that if anyone could pull off a miracle, he could.

Before leaving, he promised to call me daily with progress reports. Most sales people say they will follow up, but few ever do. Terry was different. Every night he would set his alarm for 3:00 a.m. to coordinate a conference call between his translator in Boston and the factory in Japan. These were not simple updates or casual conversations; they were complex negotiations. He worked every night to shave hours off the production schedule.

He would return to sleep for a few hours, and then call to me at 9:00 a.m. He did this seven days a week for six weeks straight. His hard work paid off, and he was able to reduce the delivery date by seven days.

It should be noted that although Terry was incredibly tenacious, he was never viewed as a pest or nuisance. He had an uncanny way of getting people on his side. He was never demanding and always showed his appreciation to the people who helped him.

Two days before the ship was scheduled to arrive in the States, Terry jumped on a plane for Long Beach, California. Once he arrived, he began establishing contacts with the right people on the docks and at customs. By the time the ship pulled into the harbor, he was standing in the observation tower drinking coffee with the Port Authority Commander.

The minute his container was unloaded, he presented the proper documentation and walked the material through the system. He took a task that could have taken as three or four days and reduced it to less than two hours.

Normally the material would have been loaded on a semi and trucked across the country to his factory in Pennsylvania (3–5 days) because no commercial air carrier would handle it, due to the unusual size and weight; but Terry had a plan. He rented a truck and drove across the state line into Nevada to an independent cargo pilot willing to hall the material. Terry loaded the plane and sat in the jump seat for the six-hour flight.

In order to avoid processing delays at a major airport, he arranged to land at a small private airstrip. Prior to leaving for California, he parked a truck at the remote air field. He unloaded the material in the middle of the night and drove it to his factory.

He arrived three hours before they opened, but since he knew all of the security guards, they gladly let him in. Not only did he unload the truck himself, he moved the material through the factory, loaded it into one of the presses, and actually made a few samples to make sure everything worked properly.

To demonstrate his political intelligence and business acumen, Terry performed an insightful task: Realizing the strength of the union and the need for their support in the future, he went to the union office and filed a grievance against *himself* for performing bargaining unit work. He handed it to the stunned third-shift union steward and said, "Take it to HR when they open in the morning and they will cut you a check." Needless to say, the steward was shocked.

Terry waited until the punch press operators arrived at 7:00 a.m. and helped them run a few more samples before checking into a local hotel to shower and catch some sleep. He retuned a few hours later to make sure everything was going as planned and did not leave the factory until all the parts were completed—two days later.

The minute the products passed inspection, he loaded them on the truck and began the six-hour drive to our factory. He arrived at 4:30 a.m., parked in front of the loading dock, and took a nap until the first shift arrived.

When the receiving department opened, he unloaded the truck and carried his products directly to the inspection department. When I arrived at 9:00 a.m., he was sitting in my chair sound asleep holding an inspection report stamped with big red letters that read "PASSED."

Terry had prevailed against all odds and won. He delivered a full week ahead of schedule, thus enabling us to meet our commitments, and saving the exclusive, three-year, $6 million dollar contract for his company.

Part II: Reward

Even though he always drove himself hard, he was especially motivated on this particular occasion. Terry's company, which had been family owned for fifty years, was about to go public. The management team was going to get stock options when the IPO (Initial Public Offering) was announced, along with certain "special people" that the president deemed worthy.

Terry was fully aware of all of the problems with our account, yet he asked to be placed on it because he knew it would be the largest contract in the history of the company. He was certain that the president would reward him for his efforts if he succeeded.

Terry's timing could not have been better. The IPO was announced two weeks after he saved our account, and the president personally invited him to a special meeting at their headquarters. When he arrived in the main conference room, he was greeted with a standing ovation from everyone in attendance. The president gave a moving speech on what a great job he had done on our account.

He even went so far as to make the claim that our contract was instrumental in the success of the IPO. The crowd went wild when he announced that not only did Terry's effort save over one hundred full-time jobs in the factory, but that they would have to hire fifty new employees to keep up with our demand.

The ceremony culminated with the president presenting Terry with a beautiful plaque commemorating his achievement and a small envelope. Terry could barely contain himself. In fact, he had to go to the men's room to settle down before he could muster the courage to open it. Nothing could have prepared him for what was inside—a $50.00 gift certificate to the Outback Steak House to take his wife and three daughters to dinner.

He immediately burst into laughter. Assuming that it was a practical joke, he went directly to the president's office for his real gift. The president graciously waved him in and Terry expressed his thanks for the celebration and his gifts.

The president smiled and went back to work. Terry was not sure what to do next, so he held up the gift certificate and said, "And thanks for the "wonderful" gift." The president sensed a note of sarcasm and replied, "Don't you like steak?" Terry replied, "I had assumed that there would be a little more than a $50 gift card."

The president held out his hand and said, "If you don't want it, you can give it back." Terry decided to end their little sparing match by getting straight to the point: "I assumed that you had me drive six hours (note: Terry worked in a field office over four hundred miles away from their headquarters) to make another announcement."

The president removed his glasses, folded his arms, and said, "Well, enlighten me—why did you think I asked you to come here?"

Terry replied, "I thought you were going to discuss the IPO with me?" The president shouted, "The IPO is for MANAGEMENT, and you are NOT MANAGEMENT!"

Terry snapped, "Yeah, but you said that people who made outstanding contributions to the company would receive stock." The president stood up and said in a firm and demeaning tone, "People like my mother, my sister, and my sons." (Ironically none of these people had ever set foot in the factory.)

Depending on who's telling the story, Terry either quit or was fired, but judging from what he told the president to do with the gift card, I assume he was fired.

Disgusted and shocked, Terry got in his car and drove the six hours back home without stopping. He used the time to plan his next move, but first he had to make things right at home. For the past twenty-five years he had given his heart and soul to the company, and during the last eight weeks he barely saw his family. He called ahead and told his wife to take the kids out of school and pack for a trip to Florida.

When he arrived at home, he told an elaborate story about the celebration and how the president insisted that he take time off. While his family loaded the minivan, he showered, changed his clothes, and then got right back on the road again. They spent two wonderful weeks in the Florida sun, and he did not tell his wife the truth until they were back home and the kids were tucked into bed.

Part III: Redemption

As expected, his wife took the news hard, but her anguish was short-lived once she heard the dozens of messages on their answering machine. To show how strong his reputation was, Terry received job offers from *all* of his competitors. He was promised everything from the director of sales to vice president of operations positions.

Terry accepted an offer from a company that said, "Tell us what you want to do, and we will create a job." Terry told the owner that he wanted to stay in sales, but he wanted to have the ability to go anywhere in the country and seek out new opportunities. He asked for a 10 percent finder's fee in addition to his normal commission for all new business he found. The owner was more than happy to agree.

Terry hit the ground running, but what I found unusual was that of all of the companies in the entire country, he made his first sales call on me. I found that odd because he knew full well that I had no business for him.

Ironically, because he had done such an outstanding job at his former employer, he locked out all other competitors for three full years due to the terms of our contract. Terry knew this, so I was curious as to why he would take the time to meet me, but that was exactly what made Terry so different.

He told me that he planned on winning back our contract. I thought it was admirable, but since it was three years away, I felt his efforts were premature. Surprisingly, Terry did not see it that way.

He presented a PERT (Program Evaluation Review Technique) Chart that detailed his plan for winning the contract, broken down into thirty-six segments, one for each month. Whereas most salespeople give vague pronouncements like, "I want to earn your business," Terry presented a detailed plan on exactly how he planned on winning our contract.

Although I was impressed, I thought it was a pipe dream, but Terry was dead serious. This was not a game to him, but a well thought-out plan. I wished him well and assumed I would not hear from him for at least two years. I was wrong.

Every month for the next twenty-eight months, Terry drove four hours to our facility and stayed 2–3 days to meet with engineers, designers, production planners, quality inspectors, and even the hourly workers on the assembly line.

Everything he did was for a well-designed purpose that culminated on the twenty-ninth month when he set up a meeting in our office with all of the department heads. Although we still had six months left on our existing contract, Terry gave new meaning to the term "preemptive strike."

To begin his presentation, Terry held up a giant check and said, "The goal of today's meeting is to save you *one million dollars*."

As cheesy as this sounds, it worked. He taped the check to the wall and said, "I want to be your new supplier. I'm here to convince you to award me all of your business at the conclusion of _this_ meeting."

The two years he spent crawling around our company gave him tremendous insight. He knew more about our situation than anyone, including our senior management. He learned three important pieces of information that no one fully understood.

The first was that there were only five companies in the country that had the necessary equipment to manufacture our products, but three could not meet our rigid specifications. That left only two companies—Terry's former and current employers.

Second, his former employer had severely underestimated the complexity of our product and was losing money on our program. They were going to refuse to continue producing our products at the end of their contract unless they got a 50 percent price increase.

The third critical piece of information was that our company had to reduce our costs by at least 15 percent to stay competitive, or we would lose our major contract. We absolutely could not accept any price increases.

The bottom line was that we were in trouble and did not know it. Terry presented all of his facts in a logical order and provided impeccable documentation. By the end of the meeting, the entire management team was disheartened, which was exactly where he wanted them.

Just when he had everyone at the lowest possible point, he made the following declaration: "I can solve all of your problems today! If you move your business to my company, we will beat your current price by 20 percent and guarantee to exceed your quality standards."

A 20 percent reduction equated to millions of dollars in savings, because our demand had grown to over $12 million a year. Terry sealed the deal by committing to ship new products in less than a month if we signed a contract right then.

The room erupted into bedlam. This was unheard of on so many levels. First of all, this was not like ordering hamburgers at a fast food restaurant; we were talking about millions of dollars of precision industrial products. Second, there was a legal matter— we were still under contract to his former company.

Terry calmly stood at the front of the room and waited until the shouting stopped. He coolly addressed each issue until there were no more questions. Everyone was finally in agreement to cancel the existing contract and move all of the business to Terry's company when the head of engineering said, "I don't want to spoil the party, but before we can approve any new supplier, they must provide ten samples for inspection."

Under most circumstances, that would have been a deal breaker. The qualification process was extremely time consuming. Some programs took as long as six months to complete. The room fell silent.

Terry's response was so good that it almost seemed rehearsed. He smiled as he dialed three numbers into the speaker phone on the conference table. The person on the other end said, "QC, how can I help you?" Terry responded, "Robert, this is Terry. Can you please give us an update?" There was a brief pause before Robert said, "All *twenty* passed with flying colors—they are the best we have ever seen."

It turned out that Terry began making samples months in advance of the meeting. He drove in the night before and worked with the QC inspectors on the second and third shifts. He knew the answer before we asked the question.

Terry then presented a copy of our contract that his president had already signed and handed it to the director of purchasing and said, "We can begin shipping next week." The director signed on the spot. By canceling our contract early, we not only saved over a million dollars, all of our quality problems instantly disappeared.

So what was Terry's reward this time?

The owner did not throw a party or give him a gift card to the Outback, but I'm sure Terry was able to buy lots of steaks with the check he received for $1,200,000. Not only did the owner not attempt to renege on his agreement, he was more than pleased to write the check because it meant an additional $12,000,000 in new business for his company.

Just when I thought I knew him, Terry shocked me one more time. I don't know how most people would react after receiving a million dollar check, but I know what I would have done.

Terry, on the other hand, took the morning off to go to the bank and pay off his mortgage, set up college funds for his daughters, and took his wife out to lunch. He was back in his office by two thirty prospecting for new customers.

Section 3

Epilogue

Chapter 11

Epilogue

As I said in the beginning, I began this journey for selfish reasons—I wanted to learn what it took to become a successful small business owner. I never dreamed of the lessons I would learn along the way. My beliefs about success going into this project were simple. I though that all you had to do was work hard and have a great product to be successful. I have to admit that I could not have been more wrong.

Although this book focused on the trials and tribulations of small business enterprises, little effort has been made to explain the benefits of ownership. My goal was to educate and inform. As one of my favorite mentors told me,

> *"My goal is not to make you feel good; my goal is to make you successful."*

That being said, there is absolutely nothing in the business world that compares with the feeling of exhilaration when a plan comes together and a business is successful. The sheer joy of success is more precious than any monetary rewards.

www.ingramcontent.com/pod-product-compliance
Lightning Source LLC
Chambersburg PA
CBHW051547170526
45165CB00002B/918